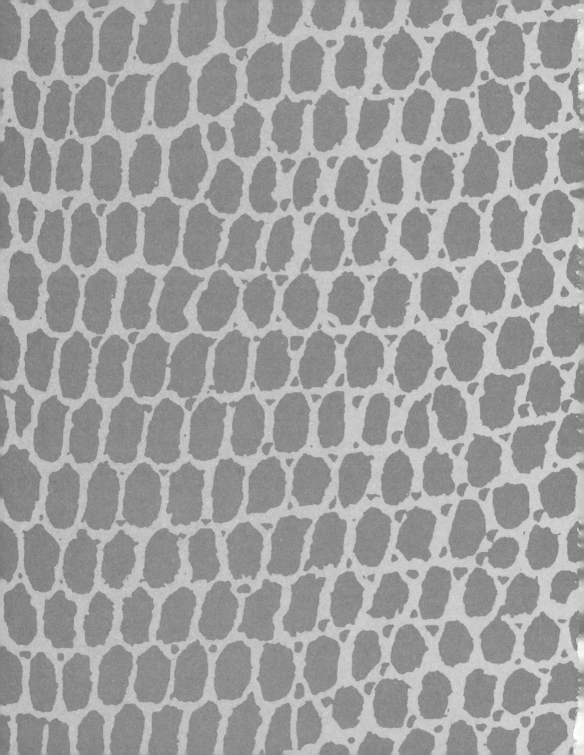

# Aquarium
# Care of
# Oscars

**NEAL PRONEK & BRIAN M. SCOTT**

*Aquarium Care of Oscars*

*Project Team*
Editor: Neal Pronek & Brian M. Scott
Copy Editor: Mary Connell
Design: Laura J. Bongarzone
Series Design: Stephanie Krautheim

*T.F.H. Publications*
President/CEO: Glen S. Axelrod
Executive Vice President: Mark E. Johnson
Publisher: Christopher T. Reggio
Production Manager: Kathy Bontz

T.F.H. Publications, Inc.
One TFH Plaza
Third and Union Avenues
Neptune City, NJ 07753

*Discovery Communications, Inc. Book Development Team*
Maureen Smith, Executive Vice President & General
  Manager, Animal Planet
Carol LeBlanc, Vice President, Marketing and Retail
  Development
Elizabeth Bakacs, Vice President, Creative Services
Peggy Ang, Director, Animal Planet Marketing
Caitlin Erb, Marketing Associate

Printed and bound in China
06 07 08 09 10  1 3 5 7 9 8 6 4 2

Library of Congress Cataloging-in-Publication Data
Pronek, Neal.
Aquarium care of oscars / Neal Pronek & Brian M. Scott.
p. cm.
Includes bibliographical references and index.
ISBN 0-7938-3762-6 (alk. paper)
1. Oscar (Fish) I. Scott, Brian M. II. Title.
SF458.O83P76 2006
639.3'774–dc22
2006013109

This book has been published with the intent to provide accurate and authoritative information in regard to the subject matter within. While every precaution has been taken in preparation of this book, the author and publisher expressly disclaim responsibility for any errors, omissions, or adverse effects arising from the use or application of the information contained herein. The techniques and suggestions are used at the reader's discretion and are not to be considered a substitute for veterinary care. If you suspect a medical problem consult your veterinarian.

*The Leader In Responsible Animal Care For Over 50 Years!™*
www.tfhpublications.com

# Table of Contents

# Introduction

Oscars are very unique and quite a treat to care for in home aquariums. Their strange, dog-like behavior and ability to recognize their owners makes them a true pet to everyone who has had the pleasure to keep them. But never underestimate the needs of oscars. They often have their own agenda, and if it doesn't agree with that of the caretaker, then problems will undoubtedly arise.

The main purpose of this book is to inform hobbyists, on all levels of experience, about what it takes to keep oscars in good health over a long period of time. Therefore, the information contained in this book is given by way of instruction for new oscar owners who feel that they could use some guidance in caring for their fish.

# Chapter 1

# Why Do You Want to Keep an

# Oscar?

The reasons why you may want to keep an oscar can be many, but one of them stands out among the rest as probably the most common reason given by oscar keepers—their personality. That's right, oscars have a "personality," and it's a good thing they do, because at first glance, it would appear that oscars don't have much going for them, especially when you compare the oscar to the copious numbers of other fishes available to hobbyists.

They're not especially colorful or graceful, they're too big for most hobbyists' tanks, they can be bullies and tough to feed, and to top it off, they're messy eaters and even greater messer-uppers of their tank's decor. So, why are oscars consistently sought after by hobbyists who know them and their ways? The answer is simple—they're just plain interesting, big, and downright popular!

### Oscars are Interesting!

Oscars are more interesting than other fishes because of their almost human-like behavior. Watch an oscar rearrange gravel and rockwork in his tank to suit himself, resisting your most determined efforts to put things where *you* want them, and you've watched an example of near-human stubbornness. This very willfulness is interesting.

Watch oscars fight or threaten over possession of something and you've seen a display of bully-ragging and braggadocio that would be the envy of any human troublemaker, and again, it's interesting.

### Oscars are Big!

In addition to having such a unique personality, probably oscars' size has a lot to do with their attractiveness, too. While oscars grow far too large for many of today's most popularly sized aquariums, this very trait is often what makes them so attractive to many hobbyists in the first place. Mature oscars are big fish by aquarium standards, adults may reach or exceed 12 inches (30 cm) in total length (TL) in less than two years, and it's tough not to catch their act, whereas the action of smaller species often goes unnoticed. Ounce for ounce of body weight, for example, the convict cichlid *(Cryptoheros nigrofasciatus)* will move a lot more gravel than an oscar, but the convict cichlid at its largest is but a fraction of a mature oscar's size and therefore may go un-watched, whereas the actions of an oscar are un-mistakable and bound to attract attention.

### Oscars are Popular!

Regardless of the reasons for it, oscars definitely are popular. Adult oscars make excellent show fish in dealers' aquariums, and mature specimens, while not the most

*Oscars may not be very colorful but their unique personalities make them popular.*

*Large adult oscars, like this red tiger oscar, can be a considerable investment.*

expensive fish in aquarium shops, are commonly right up near the top price when compared to other show fishes of equal size. And one huge difference between mature oscars and other large species is that oscars usually sell with little difficulty, while other fishes like giant pacu (*Colossoma* spp.) and clown knifefish (*Notopterus* spp.) may sit in the store for quite a while before a buyer decides to dedicate the space required for such less-interesting fishes.

## Oscars as an Investment

With the charm of the oscar pretty much summed up as far as its popularity among aquarium hobbyists is concerned, it should be mentioned that not only are these fish big, smart, and interesting, but they also happen to be one of the money-making fishes of the hobby, that is, a species worth keeping and hopefully breeding and raising the babies to sell to fellow oscar lovers or pet shops.

This last point is important in determining the popularity of a species. Many a baby oscar has been sold on the basis of the notion in its purchaser's mind that it will grow up to be able to help support his or her hobby by breeding oscars, raising their fry, and selling them off. In fact, many an adult oscar, or group of adult oscars, has been the object of considerable investment in money and in tank space on the premise that they would soon pay for themselves by the babies they produce. Oscars, however, are not that easy to breed, and hopefully you will buy your oscars with the intent to provide a loving home for them to grow and flourish under your care, not simply to turn a nickel on them.

## Oscars Defined

The fish most commonly known to American aquarium hobbyists as the oscar is also known to them as the peacock cichlid and the velvet cichlid. The names peacock cichlid and velvet cichlid are actually more common and better known in Europe, specifically in Great Britain, but all three names (and a few others, too) have achieved a degree of currency in all English-speaking lands.

## Common Name Confusion

The name "oscar" is neither descriptive nor strictly apropos in any other way, but it has stuck. It's unknown for sure how a fish like this had the name "oscar" tagged onto it, but this name has been around in the aquarium hobby for as long as the fish itself. Probably the name "oscar" is derived from a term that an early importer of tropical fishes placed on it for reasons of his own, or is some corruption of its scientific name, or perhaps "oscar" is even some local South American name that was given to it for unknown reasons. The common name of peacock cichlid is descriptive of oscars in that they are indeed cichlids, and adult oscars indeed bear at least one marking in common with a peacock, the

dark spot surrounded by a circle of lighter color near the base of the oscar's tail. This spot is referred to as an *ocellus* (plural: *ocelli*), and is similar to the eyespots that are found on a peacock's tail. In some oscars, specifically those from Peru, there may be many ocelli running just along the top of the oscar's body, and multiple caudal ocelli at the base of the oscar's tail fin.

The velvet cichlid name, probably derived from the comparative small-ness of this fish's scales, is also descriptive but to a much lesser degree; the velvety look of an adult oscar, although present if you're inclined to look for such things, is much less evident than the eyespot.

## Scientific Name of Oscars

The common oscar is known to science as *Astronotus ocellatus*. *Astronotus* means being marked with a star, and *ocellatus* means bearing an eyespot.

## The Oscar Family

The fishes within *Astronotus* belong to the family Cichlidae, which comprises some 3,200 species worldwide. Cichlidae is a group of almost completely freshwater fishes found mainly in the Americas and Africa, with a small representation in Asia. No one fully knows just how many cichlids there are because new species are being discovered all the time, and the geographical range of both African and American cichlids is far from exhaustively explored.

Until recently, the name *Astronotus ocellatus* has been used when conversing about all oscars. There are, however, two distinct and defined species, *A. ocellatus* and *A. crassipinnis*. In addition, at least a few more species remain undescribed to date. Perhaps the most notable of these new species is a variant from Argentina that appears to closely resemble a captive bred red tiger oscar, but it comes from the wild like that!

Other possible species exist as well. Another striking *Astronotus* comes from São Paulo, Brazil. This fish is most

## Oscar Origins

The natural range of wild *Astronotus ocellatus* is throughout the Amazon River drainage in northern South America while that of *A. crassipinnis* is more southern and western. Both species inhabit slow-moving waters where they hide in and among root tangles, submerged structures, and under overhanging branches. They feed voraciously on all manner of prey but especially relish insects, insect larvae, and small fishes. Today, not only are oscars found in their native waters but they can also be found in various other tropical and subtropical arenas. For example, the system of canals in southern Florida is teeming with oscars, as are several other waterways in southern Florida.

similar to *A. crassipinnis* but appears to have the orange coloration of *A. ocellatus*, too. Some professionals have estimated that Astronotus will contain about six species after its final revision is completed sometime in the near future.

## Unique Behavior of Oscars

I have already covered the charm and human-like behavior of oscars. But that's just the beginning of oscar behavior. There's a lot more that makes these fish tick, and intelligence, as well as aggression, are both huge aspects of the unique behaviors that oscars exhibit.

## Intelligence in Oscars

Apart from the morphological differences that have set cichlids apart from other fishes, they all share one trait in varying degrees that has made them, as a group, more popular than they otherwise would be—they're smarter than most other aquarium fishes. By this, it's implied that they're comparatively smarter, since they show more purposive actions than most other aquarium fishes. They seem to be a good deal more aware of what's going on around them.

If you were to compare the actions of a group of oscars with those of a group of zebra danios, tiger barbs, or neon tetras, you would know exactly what is implied by "personality" in a fish. The seemingly mindless, frenetic pacing of the barbs, danios, and tetras contrasts vividly with the actions of the cichlids that move more slowly but with far greater determination from place to place in their tank. Other fishes dash about—cichlids explore! Oscars are not alone in their capacity to be trained to perform simple tricks like ringing a bell to obtain food, but they seem to take to teaching more readily, and with greater

enjoyment, than other species. They have a greater degree of awareness of their keepers than most other fishes, and they are one of the very few piscine species that seem even remotely able to respond to human affection in any way.

In this regard, oscars reign supreme in the freshwater aquarium world. They, and certain other large cichlids, are the closest beings to animals we

*This oscar is flaring his gills as a sign that he is quite annoyed.*

*These oscars are testing each other's strength.*

normally consider to be true pets—as opposed to just interesting subjects of observation—that the freshwater aquarium hobby produces. It should be noted, however, that certain seawater fishes, most notably some grouper and batfish species, actually rival or surpass oscars in the capacity to respond to human beings.

Oscars can make fine pets. They have been known to seek out friendly hands placed in their tanks, languorously brushing themselves against the hobbyist's hands much in the same way that a dog approaches to be petted, and it has often been claimed that they can differentiate between their keepers and other people—behavior like that is decidedly un-fishlike, and it has helped to make the oscar one of the perennially most sought after of aquarium species worldwide.

## Aggressiveness in Oscars

One important aspect of the oscar's behavior pattern has to do with the fish's deportment towards other fishes that inhabit the same aquarium. Although it has often been said that the oscar is mean or even vicious, it's fair to say that compared to such beasts as piranhas and tigerfishes, the oscar is not in the least vicious. Oscars are not the most even-tempered of fishes, and they definitely have a tendency to bully tankmates of smaller size, but they are not out-and-out vicious.

Like any fish, they will eat any other fish that is able to fit in their mouths. Granted, what we think is too large for the oscar and what the oscar may think is too large may be two different things. Oscars may lord it over smaller tankmates that are too large to be eaten (for now), cooping them up in the aquarium's corners and preventing them from coming out to get their share of food, but they don't go around with the single-minded purpose of destroying every other fish they en-counter, the way some other species do. If they get their own way with other fishes they'll usually let matters rest at that point, not pursuing things to the point of outright killing. Truly mean-tempered, belligerent oscars are found, but not very often. An exception to this general rule is the temperament of the fish under spawning conditions. Mismated pairs sometimes fight to the death, with the bigger fish almost always being the killer. And oddly

enough, aggressiveness in oscars decreases as the fish grow older and larger; juvenile oscars are generally more belligerent than mature fish.

Oscars can be maintained in aquariums housing other fishes, provided the others are too large to be eaten or effectively bullied. Suitable tankmates would include large catfishes and other cichlids of a size comparable to that of the oscars; big barbs such as full-size tinfoil barbs also will get along with oscars, and so will

*Who can resist the charm of an adult oscar?*

## Aquarium Watching is Good for You!

Unfortunately, stress is a part of our lives but how we manage stress is just as important as how we try to prevent it. Finding various relaxation techniques is one way to help alleviate stress build-up and very few techniques work better than sitting in front of a large aquarium and watching the fish swim by.

While caring for any pet has proven to reduce stress and decrease hypertension, aquariums are particularly effective at this. In fact, many doctor's and dentist's offices have at least one aquarium situated in the waiting room for patients to observe before they meet with the physician.

Studies have shown that displaying aquaria of brightly colored fishes actually curtailed the often disruptive behaviors of Alzheimer patients and increased their appetites as well. Other studies have proven that aquariums can actually calm children diagnosed with attention deficit/hyperactivity disorder (ADHD).

big characoid types such as the *Anostomus* and *Leporinus* species. Even combining large silver dollars of the genera *Metynnis* and *Myleus* with oscars will often work in very large aquariums. More detailed coverage of suitable tankmates for oscars will be presented further along in this book.

### A Face Only a Mother Could Love

By and large, oscars are not physically attractive. Their scales don't shimmer, their fins don't flow gracefully behind them (Even veil-tailed oscars have rather stiff and ragged fins.). Their large, bug-like eyes seem to protrude in such a way as to make them appear like some creature that one would encounter in a bar scene in a sci-fi movie. Nevertheless, people are fanatical about these monsters and are fascinated with them in all their glory.

### Relaxation & Fascination

Oscars exhibit a determination that is nothing short of fascinating. If you've ever been privileged enough to have seen a large aquarium with just a few mature adult oscars roaming about in it, then you'll understand completely. Their graceful moving and back-and-forth slow swimming is reminiscent of watching large groupers in a giant public aquarium display tank, only the oscars are usually a lot smaller than groupers, thankfully! That doesn't matter though. Watching an oscar, or better yet a small group of oscars,

*A beautifully colored red oscar is always a true showpiece.*

hobbyists to set up and effectively maintain a couple of large oscars, a few large Amazon sword-plants, some bogwood, a nice gravel bottom, and perhaps even a few other types of fishes to keep the oscars company. Such a display tank would be quite impressive to say the least, and best of all—it's possible!

explore their aquatic domain is quite fascinating and very relaxing, too.

## A Slice of Nature

Recently, there has been an increase in the interest in aquariums simply because of the connection that one feels with nature when an aquarium is present in his or her home or office. There is little question as to whether or not a slice of an Amazonian rainforest is a beautiful thing—of course it is! And to be able actually to care for such a unique, albeit man-made, piece of nature is nothing short of impressive. A large aquarium, say over 100 gallons (378 l), allows

## Having Fun with Your Oscar

It is very possible to enjoy a single oscar without trying to breed them or without an elaborate and fancy setup. In fact, some of the great oscar scholars have been those hobbyists who kept only one specimen at a time. An individual oscar that is kept becomes as much a member of the family as any dog or cat, and these hobbyists are the ones who probably have the most fun with their fish.

While a single oscar can easily be raised to adulthood in a 50- or 75-

SMALL FRY

## Differences in Appearance Caused By Age

A consideration entirely different from that of color variation between strains of oscars is taking into account the difference in appearance between baby wild-type oscars and juvenile wild-type oscars and between juvenile wild-type oscars and adult wild-type oscars. Baby wild-type oscars are a deep brown, almost black, with an irregular network of creamy streaks all over the body. As the babies grow, the streaks gradually disappear and are replaced by the basic brownish-red adult coloration. Juvenile wild-type oscars are less colorful than adults and lack the ocellus (or ocelli), but they couldn't be mistaken for anything but oscars, whereas babies are often thought to be a different species altogether. The differences between the life stages of other strains of oscars are not as pronounced. For example, a juvenile red oscar is very similar to an adult red oscar and the same is true for the albino oscars, lemon oscars, and red tiger oscars.

gallon (189 to 284 l) aquarium, the attention paid to them is really the most critical variable here compared to the size of the aquarium in which they are housed. Such an individual fish will surely get a lot of attention paid to it. For example, the hobbyist often greets the fish when he or she first comes home, and the oscar may even have special time set aside for it in the evenings. In some instances, pet oscars have been known to be treated like children and receive special treats on their "birthdays"—the yearly anniversary of the day the oscar was brought home. Holidays are often special times for the pet oscar, and since oscars eat basically anything that's edible, they often get some of the Thanksgiving turkey, too. The proper diet of oscars will be covered in great detail later in this book, so please don't feed your oscar *any* of the Thanksgiving turkey!

Although some oscars are spoiled and treated like children—at least an oscar won't need a college education or ask to borrow the family car. But, speaking of education…

## Oscar Trick Training

As smart as oscars are, it must be remembered that they still have a primitive brain, so it's important to keep the tricks simple. Even so, oscars will amaze people who don't know that a fish can even think, let alone do a trick or two. In attempting to train an oscar, it's important to keep in mind the behavior that you eventually want to elicit from the trick and then decide how you're going to go about getting that behavior.

The first step in attempting to train an oscar to perform a trick or two is to utilize a small bell or clicker. Ring the bell, or click the clicker, whenever you feed the fish. Eventually, your fish will come to associate that sound with an offering of food. And it's easier to reward a behavior performed after a signal, such as a bell, than it is with the actual food itself.

## Trick #1:
### Swimming Through a Submerged Hoop

For example, if you were going to teach your fish to swim through a hoop, then start with placing the hoop in the water. The oscar would surely examine it, and eventually may stick its head part way through the hoop. So, then ring the bell and reward him with a small piece of food whenever he does that. This may go on for several days and the oscar will usually get the idea that he gets foods whenever he stick his head in the hoop. After a few more days, to encourage the oscar not only to stick his head in the hoop but to actually swim through it, try to place food in the tank in such a way as to force him to go through the hoop to get at it. If he does not swim all the way through the hoop, then simply withhold food and walk away. Usually, after a few times of trial and error, the oscar will get the hint that something just isn't right and may try swimming through the hoop. When this happens, reward him with food. It may be a back-and-forth for a while but usually within a week or so he will get the hint that just the head-in-the-hoop doesn't suffice any longer.

## Trick #2:
### The Making of a "Watch Oscar"

Some hobbyists like to have an oscar that acts like a watchdog, hitting the front glass and acting aggressive and belligerent—especially toward people. That is easily accomplished; in fact,

*Oscars are usually protective of their territories.*

*Remember that oscars are big fish, and they can cause quite a stir in the tank when they get upset.*

some oscars demonstrate this behavior without any training at all. It only takes a little encouragement for the oscar to demonstrate his natural propensity to protect his territory. Go up to the glass and shake your head back and forth to mimic a challenging fish and then back away as the oscar approaches. Do this for a little while each day and you'll be quite surprised how soon you have yourself a "watch oscar" on your premises. Just don't expect him to bark!

### Trick #3:
### Petting Your Oscar

The trick most people want their oscar to perform is to allow the hobbyist to actually pet him. Although this is perhaps the most common trick, it's among the least natural behavior for the oscar to learn. First, it must be realized that oscars have no natural desire to allow themselves to be petted. On the contrary, it's fairly natural for most dogs and cats to want to be petted, and such traits are actually enhanced through selective breeding over many generations. So, in the case of your oscar, you are going to need to provide lots of time, attention, and incentives (in the form of food of course) to get your oscar to allow himself to be petted.

Most of the people who have gotten their oscars to accept being petted have first started off with short, quick brushes against the fish's scales. It may start when cleaning the aquarium; as the oscar swims by, simply stick a finger or two toward him and briefly touch him. Sometimes, the hobbyist will set out to deliberately establish this behavior. What it amounts to is that

*Sometimes tricks are less effective if more than one oscar is housed in the same aquarium.*

the fish tolerates the touching and isn't spooked off by it because he has become used to it. That translates into lots of practice and starting things off very slowly. It also helps to reward the fish with food, of course. In fact, sometimes the behavior is an outgrowth of hand-feeding your oscar. Teaching oscars to eat from your hand is as easy as falling off a log. Once you get them used to that, they begin to associate your hands with food and are therefore more willing to be touched by them. Just be sure to touch them very gently at first and be very cautious not to spook the fish, as

doing so will lead to more trouble and a longer road to being able to pet them in the end. Patience, as always, is the emphasis here.

### Oscar Toys

Aquarium shops display a number of decorations, from small boats to rocking chairs to small glass or plastic spheres for aquariums. Taking into account an oscar's natural inclination to explore things, and to mouth them, it is not surprising that oscars actually like having something new that they can toss around placed in their tanks each week. Just be sure to remove the old one and make sure that what you put in the tank has no harmful parts or chemicals on it that can cause harm to the fish.

The point here is that oscars are highly curious fish, and they enjoy having something new put into the tank that they can examine and toss around. Of course, this doesn't mean that you have to buy a new toy for them each week. Just get four or five items and rotate them through the tank weekly. Not only is it fun to watch the oscar play with them, but the habit of providing the fish with toys may actually increase their intelligence. Studies with rats utilizing an enriched environment of new toys each week indicated that rats that experienced enrichment with fresh toys actually had a larger brain mass compared to rats that were deprived of toys. And oscars live a lot longer than rats.

## Oscars; The Family Pet?

For some people, keeping an oscar is like keeping a family pet, and they would no more think of breeding oscars than they would have a kennel of dogs. Even so, these persons may be excellent scholars of the oscar. But when watching these folks with their family pets, it is sometimes difficult to tell just who is studying whom! For others, the real enjoyment in keeping oscars is to breed them and be able to observe their parental instincts and the way that they raise and care for their young. Whichever type you are, you will certainly find that oscars are intriguing fish indeed. It is not without reason that the very personable and affable oscar has maintained such prominence in the tropical fish hobby for so long.

## Oscar Office Tanks

It's not uncommon for business owners or office managers to set up a large aquarium in a carefully selected spot—only to be uncertain as to what to put in it. Oscars of course! Oscars are perfect for large office tanks. Their active and curious demeanor coupled with their large size makes them ideal candidates for show tanks.

If you choose an oscar or two for your office show tank, be sure to provide the proper filtration and water circulation that such big fish need. Oscars can be messy when improperly kept, so make sure to pay close attention to the following chapters so you can have a beautiful, thriving oscar office tank.

# Chapter 2

# Getting Your Tank Started &

# Keeping it Running

Aside from a great personality, oscars possess a hardiness that is tough to match, and they do very well in aquariums as long as some basic requirements are met. One of these requirements is the initial selection of their home—the aquarium. The selection and setup of an aquarium destined to house an oscar is very important and a certain amount of general aquarium knowledge is required in order to make this important decision, and make it right the first time.

## Aquarium Selection

In general, a big fish needs a big tank, and the oscar is no exception. As a matter of fact, on an inch-for-inch of body-length basis, the oscar needs even more space than most other aquarium fishes. Oscars are bulky, not streamlined like so many other fishes, and they often create such a mess when they are feeding—therefore both of these conditions dictate providing extra space for the fish involved.

Under ideal conditions, a fish will initially be given as much tank space as it would require at its full size. This general rule is rarely applied in actual practice. What usually happens is that the hobbyist takes a fancy to a fish and then buys the fish regardless of what it needs, hoping that all will go well even though he is unable to provide sufficient room. This is completely unfair to the poor fish.

You might be able to successfully house a 2-in. (5-cm) oscar in a 10-gallon (38-liter) aquarium, but what happens when he grows to 3 in. (7.5 cm) or 4 in. (10 cm) or even 5 in. (12.5 cm)? Then what? You'll quickly be in need of another tank, so you might as well start with the correct size.

Small oscars are commonly put into tanks that contain other species. Of course, as the oscar grows, it will systematically eliminate most of the tankmates that stay small, and tankmates that match the oscar in growth shouldn't be housed with it in the first place if you intend to allow enough space for the oscar's optimum growth.

Whatever monetary outlay you expend for space is well worth it, so don't stint on tank size. If you have a 50-gallon (190-liter) aquarium and want to use it to house an interesting fish, an oscar may be just what you're looking for. If you have a 75-gallon (285-liter) aquarium and not only want to house a big fish but maybe would like a shot at

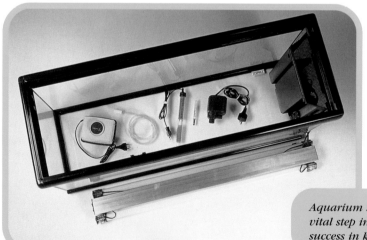

*Aquarium selection is a vital step in your ultimate success in keeping oscars.*

spawning a pair of oscars, then they may give you your chance. A tank of the proper size not only is a major factor in keeping your fish healthy, it also provides a margin of safety for them when conditions start to go bad.

## Aquarium Placement & Stand Selection

Even the smallest of aquaria are generally considered heavy by comparison to the weight of equally sized objects. To provide the support that your aquarium needs, you will need to make some arrangements to have a stand that will hold the weight of the aquarium. Aquarium stands themselves can be quite heavy, which will, of course, add to the overall weight and pressure being exerted on your floor.

### Check for Electricity

Before we go any further, take a look at the location where you're considering placing your tank setup. Check to see that there are sufficient electrical

*Aquarium placement is the next important step to success.*

outlets next to it. They should be protected by a ground fault circuit interrupter (GFCI) device, since you are dealing with electricity in the vicinity of water.

### Check the Floor

Once you have chosen a spot that has electricity but no direct sunlight, you are ready to check the most important thing of all—the floor! Your floor should be solid. If you are fortunate enough to have a concrete slab under the chosen area—great; if not, make sure the floor is able to hold the combined weight of the aquarium setup. Remember, the tank with all of its equipment is going to be far heavier than what most people can readily pick up by themselves. Add water at 8.3 pounds per gallon for fresh water, and you have yourself a seriously heavy piece of furniture.

A solid floor may be first in importance to support your aquarium, but a solid stand is definitely a close second. Unless you are a good

25

carpenter or know someone who is, stay away from homemade aquarium stands. In addition, many manufacturers offer warranties if you buy both an aquarium and a stand from them. This combination is by far the most highly recommended route to take.

Regardless of the stand you choose, pay close attention to how evenly balanced the aquarium is when placed on top of it. Companies that build such stands test them prior to shipping them to your local aquarium shop, but it never hurts to check for yourself. After all, sometimes the stand may have been used to support other things that are far heavier than what the stand was initially rated to hold, or the stand may have come in contact with excessive moisture or temperature extremes. These are factors that can significantly affect the structural integrity of the stand.

## Check the Level

Once you have positioned your stand and placed your aquarium on it, use a level to make sure the tank sits perfectly even on all sides. Even a slight lean due to an uneven floor or the like can cause disaster to strike in the form of a cracked panel or broken seam. If the tank and stand are slightly uneven, this can be fixed prior to adding water by using wooden shims or foam board placed in the proper areas to offset the problem. Some hobbyists have used foam as a cushion placed in between the tank and stand just in case there are small inconsistencies that

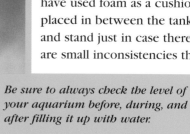

*Be sure to always check the level of your aquarium before, during, and after filling it up with water.*

## Power Filters are Preferred

There are countless numbers of brands, models, and types of filters available to the oscar keeper and choosing the one that's right for your setup can be an exhausting feat to say the least. Of this vast assortment, power filters reign supreme. This is mainly due to the ease with which they can be operated and the availability, and assortment, of filter materials that can be used in them. Power filters offer the oscar keeper many options and a flexibility that is just not found in other forms of filtration. Additionally, power filters often provide increased circulation, which is also very critical in maintaining the health of your oscar. A visit to your favorite pet retailer can show just how many examples there are for your review before you make your choice.

cannot be readily seen with the naked eye. Such a safety precaution is recommended, though not usually needed.

### A Test Run

Once you have successfully placed your aquarium stand in the perfect location and have assured that the aquarium will sit evenly upon it, you can go about setting up the system. While actually filling the tank is not necessarily the next step, you can begin to add some water, so as to allow the stand some time to adjust to the eventual weight of the tank when full of water. During the initial filling of the tank it is common to hear the stand creak and make some other small noises. Of course, if the creaks

turn into cracks and so on, you may need to rethink your plans and adjust for whatever situation that may follow. In any instance, such noises should cause you to make draining the aquarium your first priority and seeking the assistance of a qualified aquarium technician your second.

*After the tank is level, you're ready for a test run.*

## Filtration

Filtration is a large topic. This process can be as simple or as intricate as you would like it to be, but one thing is certain: the need to understand what is happening on a microbiological level in your aquarium is vitally important. To begin gaining this understanding, we need to look at what the role of filtration actually is and where it begins. Filtration is defined as a process where a substance undergoes biological, chemical, or mechanical changes in order to enhance its purity. This definition is basic and since the topic of filtration itself is rather lengthy, we will only discuss the three main types; but first we must learn a little about a very important cycle that every aquarium, whether freshwater or marine, must undergo if any filtration is to be successful—the nitrogen cycle.

To a certain extent, the need for efficiency in filtration systems for use in aquariums housing oscars is dictated by the size of the fish; if oscars need big tanks and big tanks need good filtration systems, then oscar owners surely need big tanks with good filtration. The need for such systems is mostly dictated by the oscar's habits, especially their messy eating habits. The oscar happens to be a terribly sloppy

eater, even sloppier than just about all other aquarium fishes of equal size. Big oscars chomp and gum their food over and over again; in fact it's a wonder that any of it actually makes it down their throats! Small particles often find their way all over the tank where they lie ignored and eventually decompose.

Decomposition processes in an aquarium are potentially very dangerous. Organic substances cannot safely be left lying around in the tank; choosing a filter thus becomes a job of

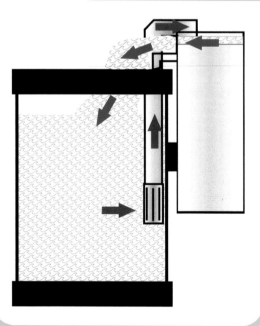

*This illustration shows a power filter in action. Red arrows indicate dirty water (in) and the blue arrows indicate clean water (out).*

## The Six Basic Elements for Success

Here's a checklist of what is considered the basic elements for success with oscars:

1. As large an aquarium as possible.
2. A strong stand to place the tank on.
3. Good, strong filtration system.
4. Sturdy cover (lighting optional).
5. Heater.
6. This book!

pumps to drive it for them, so power filters generally filter more gallons per hour and therefore do a better filtering job on large tanks. Also, they create a current in the water that seems to be beneficial to the fish; other filters also produce a current, but much less strongly. If you are housing a big oscar in a big tank, a power filter is your best bet; if you have a number of large oscars in a big tank, or a greater number of smaller oscars, a power filter is a must-have.

## Heaters

The need for an aquarium heater depends partly on the temperatures in the area where you live and partly on your style of raising fishes, as well as on the size of the tank(s). Some hobbyists who raise oscars never have any real

picking out the unit that will remove most of the subject-to-decay organic materials in the tank.

In a small aquarium, under 10 gallons (37.8 l) in capacity, you can often get away with a small filtration unit, say an inside sponge filter or a small hang-on style power filter. Once you get into the realm of larger aquariums, and larger oscars, the best filtration is obtained through the use of external power filters. Power filters push the water directly, rather than relying on air

29

*Oscars prefer warm temperatures.*

need for an aquarium heater, since the temperatures in their area never fall to a lethal level. Oscars can get by at 70°F even though this temperature is considered too low for them to exhibit good growth. A temperature that remains a degree or two upward or downward of 76°F would be much better, with breeding temperatures about 5 degrees higher. In subtropical areas like Hawaii and southern Florida, oscars can be maintained outdoors permanently. In warmer temperate areas, which for our purposes here will be defined as those circumstances where an unheated pool containing 500 gallons or more in capacity would not fall below 65°F for more than a day or so during the summer months, oscars can safely be kept outside; the large quarters thus afforded will do them lots of good. Young oscars will grow much more quickly, with less attention, if maintained in a large outdoor raising pool, but they'll probably get a bit ragged looking as well.

In general, the best recommendation about the purchase of heating equipment is to get the best, or at least close to the best, and make sure that it's powerful enough to heat the biggest tank in which it may be used. You might not need a heater at all if the place in which you keep the oscar tank wouldn't allow an unheated tank to fall below 68°F for more than a few days at most, but you would certainly need one if you wanted to raise your water's temperature to between 80° and 85°F in a place that barely goes over 75°F. Whatever type of heater you choose, make sure that it can be securely anchored in place; a large oscar can easily knock a loose heater out of the tank, a prospectively very dangerous situation. Completely submergible heaters are the best choices in general but are comparatively expensive.

## Lighting

Aquarium reflectors serve two major purposes: they provide light for live plants and light for the aquarist to

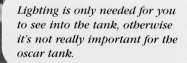

*Lighting is only needed for you to see into the tank, otherwise it's not really important for the oscar tank.*

see into the tank. If you don't have live plants in the tank and it receives enough incidental light to enable you to see into it, you don't need an actual aquarium light at all—especially since oscars don't like bright light. If the oscar tank happens to be a decorative feature of your house, you'll want it illuminated, but don't let the light become glaring. Whether the lighting fixture is incandescent or fluorescent makes no difference to the fish, but red oscars seem to show up best under fluorescent fixtures designed for good plant growth.

## Tank Decor

An oscar aquarium need not be outfitted from front to back and side to side with fancy decorations. In fact, some of the most spectacular display aquariums housing oscars barely have any decorations in them at all. They show off the fish, not the aquascaping. Many oscar owners either use totally bare aquariums or those where only rockwork has been added. Bare tanks, of course, don't look overly nice to most people, but they're fine as an environment for simply allowing an oscar to grow or for letting a wounded oscar heal, or maybe even for oscars in quarantine awaiting transport to their final show tank.

### Rockwork

Oscar owners who are concerned about the aesthetic appeal of their

# Importance of Water Changes

One of the most important points in maintaining good water quality in your oscar's aquarium is making partial water changes on a regular basis. This basic element in successful aquarium maintenance is not stressed as heavily as it should be. Aquarium books often do not place enough emphasis on it; fish dealers don't always harp on it as they should; and experienced hobbyists may forget to point out how important they are to beginners when giving them advice. But water changes are immensely important, and making frequent partial water changes is the single most positive action an oscar owner can take to insure the good health of his or her fish.

Water changes improve color (because healthy fish show better color than unhealthy fish), improve growth, improve behavior, assist in resisting disease, keep the aquarium cleaner and clearer, and they promote spawning activity. In short, water changes provide many advantages with no disadvantages, unless you consider the time and effort spent performing them a disadvantage. It doesn't matter what type of magnificent and elaborate type of filtration unit you are using on your oscar's tank— nothing beats water changes!

oscar tank can use a wide assortment of rocks to decorate the tank. Although quite a few rocks can serve this purpose, since many are readily available, decorative, while also not too expensive nor harmful from the standpoint of affecting the water quality adversely, various types of shale happen to be the rock choice for many oscar owners. It's the most common and least costly of all the rock types sold in aquarium stores, and it can be very attractive if arranged artistically in the tank. If you have neither the talent nor inclination to create shale arrangements for your tank, you can usually find some ready-made rock shapes. They often come in the form of cliffs and ledges and caves, among other fabricated shapes, but probably the most common are the various shale backgrounds that cover the entire back of the tank. Thankfully, many of these are also made from foam so the weight of the shale is no longer a factor.

## Bogwood

Another form of decor commonly employed in oscar setups is bogwood, also referred to as driftwood. This material is collected from various habitats all over the world and then subjected to a strict cleaning and preparation regimen. Finally, after sometimes weeks of preparation, the wood is dried then exported to its final destinations.

Bogwood often leeches tannins into the tank's water giving it a tea-like appearance. This is fine and no harm is done by these tannins. One slight side effect is that the wood often softens the water and thus the pH may drop to a level that is not safe. Care should be

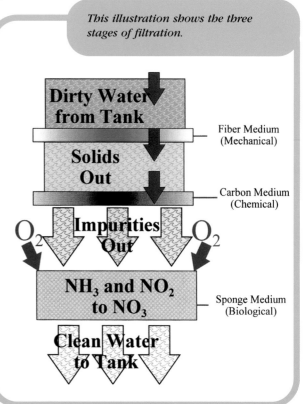

This illustration shows the three stages of filtration.

Dirty Water from Tank

Fiber Medium (Mechanical)

Solids Out

Carbon Medium (Chemical)

$O_2$ Impurities Out $O_2$

$NH_3$ and $NO_2$ to $NO_3$

Sponge Medium (Biological)

Clean Water to Tank

*Test your water's chemistry on a weekly basis.*

nitrogen and oxygen.

There are several steps involved here, and each one will be touched on specifically. For now, however, it is important to understand that such a process does take place and is the primary reason that you aren't able to dump a large amount of fish into your aquarium at one time. This is especially true with new aquaria, as the "spike" of ammonia produced by the fish will quickly cause the fish a lot of discomfort and can surely kill them should the ammonia levels become uncontrollably high. For this reason, you should always take great care in breaking in, or cycling, your aquarium. To cycle your tank means to simply allow the proper bacterial species responsible for the breakdown of nitrogenous wastes enough time to develop and begin their duties. This time frame will vary, depending on many conditions, such as water temperature, volume of the aquarium, number of fish in the aquarium, amount of other biomass, pH and other water chemistry values of the tank's water, and the presence of a suitable substratum for the beneficial bacteria to colonize. The estimated time frame required to properly break

taken to monitor the pH of any aquarium containing bogwood, as it may eventually harm your oscar(s).

## Cycling Your Aquarium

The cycling, or breaking in, of any aquarium is best achieved by first having a basic understanding of the nitrogen cycle. The nitrogen cycle is the process of converting a highly toxic nitrogen compound, usually in the form of ammonia, back to pure in an aquarium is approximately four weeks. That number is simply an average and should in no way be taken as law. However, even if your tank cycles in a week, waiting a bit longer will do absolutely no harm whatsoever. There is no punishment for moving slowly while adding live animals to your tank. Feel free to add a fish each year to the tank if you would like. On the other hand, if you dump a bunch of fish in the tank and it takes two weeks to calm down, then you must not think that you can make a habit out of continuing to dump in large amounts of fish at one time. The biological backbone of the aquarium will break, and you will lose badly.

Now you should have a good idea of how the nitrogen cycle plays a huge role in the determination of your success or failure in your aquarium experiences. That said, we should attempt to get a better understanding of the inner workings of this cycle, to be able to identify the steps as they progress through the break-in process.

## Testing…Testing…1, 2, 3

Testing your oscar's aquarium water is usually going to produce the same results test after test. What follows is a general guideline as to what to test for and where to expect the results of the tests to fall in relation to a "perfect" environment.

*Oscars are not particularly sensitive to the pH of their tank as long as extremes are avoided.*

## pH

In nature, oscars are found across a wide range of habitats all having slightly different pH readings. Generally, oscars are not sensitive to this measurement as long as extremes are avoided. For example, a pH of 4.2 is far too acidic for an oscar to live in comfortably but believe it or not they can survive in it for a short time. The same can be said of a pH reading around 9.2. Such a high pH is far too basic, but an oscar, especially a big adult, will survive in it for a short time. Most oscar tanks test in at around 6.0 but by all means, try to keep the pH around neutral (7.0) if possible.

## Ammonia

Ammonia is a toxic compound of nitrogen and hydrogen. In aquariums, ammonia toxicity is the number one cause of death for aquarium fishes, and it is usually the result of overfeeding. The decaying foodstuffs decompose and give off this dangerous compound. In nature, ammonia is produced and consumed at a rate that never really allows it to become toxic to higher life forms but in aquariums, where there may be an absence of biological organisms, it can become a deadly substance in a matter of hours. In aquariums, ammonia will always be

### The Expert Knows

## Supplies to Keep on Hand

All of the tools and gadgets used in tanks housing other fishes have value for the oscar specialists, too. Thermometers, feeding rings, powerheads, air pumps, nets, siphons, and test kits all have their place. Owners of large oscars need wide, deep nets of soft fibers, although some owners of big fish never use nets at all, doing whatever oscar-transfer work that has to be done by trapping the fish in a soft towel or blanket after first removing most of the water in the tank.

present at some level but be sure that it does not go higher than 0.05 ppm, which happens to be a common result for the test in most oscar aquariums.

## Nitrite

Nitrite should be taken very seriously, for it is a highly toxic substance, and although it is albeit not so harmful as ammonia in the same concentrations, it can still easily kill oscars and other large fishes. Remember that polluted water may be crystal clear but can still hold a high concentration of harmful substances. Certain nitrifying bacteria are able to convert the ammonia into a less toxic nitrogen

*A beautiful albino red tiger oscar.*

compound called nitrite. Nitrite is odorless, so don't be fooled into believing that you can smell your water to see if it is bad. Just as in the case of ammonia, oscar tanks will always have a touch of this compound but keeping it at a manageable level is very important. A reading of 0.02 is about as high as you will want to see on a nitrite test.

## Nitrate

Nitrate is the last breakdown and least harmful product in the nitrogen cycle. From here, any nitrate that is not converted back to free nitrogen and oxygen will be used to provide nutrients to any type of photosynthetic organism that comes in contact with your water. As a matter of fact, old tank water is often used to water house plants or a garden, due to the high

levels of nitrate and other metabolites that are often found in it. Anaerobic bacteria will also consume nitrate, in which case nitrogen will be liberated, and then the cycle will be completed. Nitrate is not usually found in high concentration in natural bodies of water. Needless to say, many fish, even the hardy oscar, will only tolerate so much of it. Keeping the overall nitrate level below 50 mg/l is best, as anything higher than that may cause acute toxicity over long periods of time. Both nitrite and nitrate can be tested for through the use of a simple liquid drop or dip-strip test kit. Often, the same test kit will offer the user the ability to perform both tests at the same time. However, hobbyists looking for more exact measurements should purchase a kit that focuses solely on one or the other as an independent test.

## Plants? Don't Bother!

Small oscars can be kept in planted aquaria because small oscars usually don't bother plants. On the contrary, medium- and large-sized oscars cannot be kept in planted aquaria, unless it's an extraordinarily large tank, because medium- and large-sized oscars do bother plants. Large oscars bother rooted plants by turning them into uprooted plants. It doesn't seem to make much difference whether the plants are small or large, planted in gravel or planted in special pots; if a large oscar wants to move them, and he usually does, he will. If you want rooted plants in the tank and the oscar leaves them alone, fine. But if you want rooted plants in the tank and the oscar pulls them up as fast as you anchor them down, stop trying—unless you just want to provide entertainment for the fish or you're interested in a protracted piscine-human contest of wills.

## Keep it Covered!

Every oscar tank should have a cover and be kept covered. While oscars are not generally considered "jumpers," they will do so on occasion. Another,

*Nets are important pieces of equipment to have on hand.*

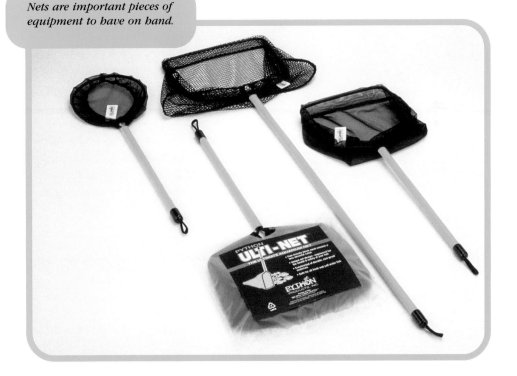

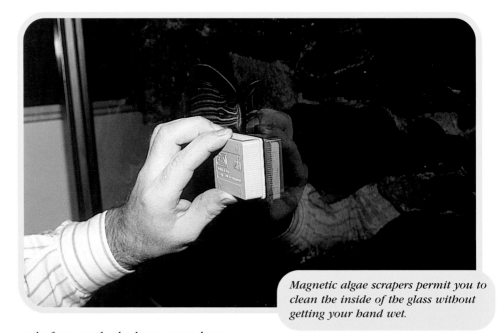

*Magnetic algae scrapers permit you to clean the inside of the glass without getting your hand wet.*

and often overlooked, reason to keep a cover on an aquarium is to keep things like dust, dirt, debris, cat's paws, and other things out of it. Most hobbyists don't realize just how much airborne dirt can get into an aquarium and with all of the pesticides, perfumes, and cleaning agents that are commonly used in and around houses this can become a problem. Oscars do like to splash water out of the tank, and a mature specimen can do quite a bit of sprinkle work by whipping its broad tail around the top of the tank. With young oscars, you can avoid jumping and splashing by simply covering the tank, but with older, heavier fish you will have to both cover it and weigh or clamp the cover down.

The following guidelines are just that, guidelines. There are many other things that need attention paid to them. And sometimes things don't go according to your schedule. For example, if you see that your canister filter is clogged after only two weeks of operation, then simply clean it. Don't wait until the schedule says that you have to; if it needs it, do it and then restart the schedule for that particular item. The maintenance of an oscar tank can be fun and exciting, and even something that can involve the whole family. If you constantly wait until the last minute, then it will become a chore and something that nobody wants to be involved in.

## The Maintenance Factor

With any aquarium, especially an oscar aquarium, comes a certain amount of maintenance that needs to be performed. This maintenance is commonly broken into three categories: daily, weekly, and monthly. Let's have a look at what it takes to keep an oscar tank up and running. Note that normal feeding does not appear on these schedules.

### Daily Maintenance

The daily maintenance of your oscar tank should consist of the following steps:

1. Wipe down the aquarium glass (both inside and outside).
2. Check the aquarium's water level.
3. Observe your oscar(s) for at least a few minutes daily.
4. Inspect all power appliances to make sure they are operating normally.
5. Check the water temperature.

### Weekly Maintenance

The weekly maintenance of your oscar tank should consist of the following procedures:

1. Perform a partial water change of at least 25% of the tank's total volume.
2. Clean gravel with a gravel-cleaning apparatus.
3. Inspect filter cartridge(s) to see if it/they need replacing.
4. Inspect hoses and aquarium seams for leakage.

5. Offer a treat in the form of live insects or fresh fish.
6. Test pH, ammonia, nitrite, and nitrate.

### Monthly Maintenance

The monthly maintenance of your oscar tank should consist of the following operations:

1. Perform a major water change consisting of approximately 50% to 65% of the aquarium's water.
2. Do a full gravel cleaning and partial replacement if needed.
3. Service filter thoroughly (not at the same time as any major water change).
4. Check air hoses and connections.
5. Replace air pump's filter.
6. Clean the impeller on any power filter or water pump.

*Gravel cleaning should be done on a weekly basis.*

# Chapter 3

# Eating Well

Foods suitable for oscars come in various forms. Many of them have been formulated into prepared specialty feeds that are offered for sale through pet retailers and local aquarium shops. These specialty feeds are probably the best way for a beginning hobbyist to provide a broad range of nutrients to their oscar, but there are also many other ways to do this.

*Juvenile oscars that are fed properly will grow very fast.*

The first thing hobbyists seeking to learn about feeding their oscar should do, whether experienced or not, is to familiarize themselves with the various forms of general fish foods that are available. It is surprising how many foods are suitable, and often of quite good quality, but are rarely used due to a lack of information on them. Another issue that concerns hobbyists is the lack of availability of many foods. This is especially true with the various live foods.

Oscars, large and small, are big eaters. In fact, they are downright gluttonous. Sometimes their excesses in consumption give them serious digestive upsets; oscars even have been known to die as the result of eating too much.

## Commercial Foods

Most commercial foods take the form of dry, packaged diets that are exclusively developed for use with aquarium or ornamental fishes. These can come in an assortment of sizes and shapes, which include pellets, granules, tablets, flakes, and chunk forms.

## Dry Foods

Dry foods vary in their ease of usage, cost, nutritive value, storage length, and other factors, but overall are a good cheap food source for tropical fishes. Unfortunately, oscars are not typical of the main run of tropical aquarium fishes, and some prepared foods just don't suit them when they get large. For small oscars, a

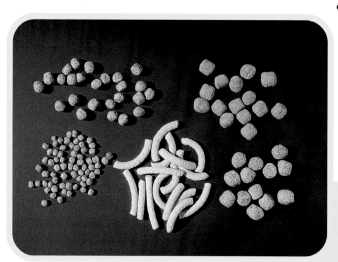

*Commercial foods come in a wide assortment of formulations.*

variety of packaged dry foods, especially meaty foods, can form the bulk of their diet, but big oscars will need chunkier items.

Some hobbyists who keep large oscars feed their fish regularly on a diet of pelleted dry foods, using mostly pellets that are marketed for pool fish, koi, or even trout. Although these diets are formulated specifically for good growth and health in salmonid and cyprinid fishes, they do have value for use as oscar feed, and some hobbyists use them without any problem. I might warn you, however, that not all oscars will accept them, so try to obtain and use only a sample supply before you stock up on them.

*Bloodworms are commonly used for feeding young ocars.*

## Frozen Foods

Daphnia, brine shrimp, bloodworms, mosquito larvae, beef heart, and a few other foods are available regularly from pet shops in frozen form. Frozen brine shrimp is by far the most common and easily obtainable, and it can be a good food for small and medium-sized oscars. It's comparatively expensive, but a given amount of frozen brine shrimp costs a lot less than the same weight in live brine shrimp would cost, that's for sure! So, the little crustaceans are a good deal more economical to feed in frozen form than they are in live form.

Frozen bloodworms are also a very good food for small and medium-sized oscars. Like brine shrimp, bloodworms are far less expensive when purchased frozen compared to live. Bloodworms are actually a form of midge larvae and not worms at all. In nature, small oscars feed very heavily on insect larvae, so bloodworms are a very natural food for them. Frozen daphnia is pretty junky stuff for any oscar older than a few weeks of age. It tends to fall apart and float around the tank only to decompose, and decomposition in any aquarium is potentially hazardous, so it's probably best to steer clear of this

*Fresh, raw shrimp can be used as a healthy alternative to live foods for oscars.*

type of frozen food.

Frozen beef heart and other slaughterhouse by-products, which can be obtained in large packages and therefore economical to use, have good food value and many oscar keepers often use them as staple items in the diet of their oscars (and some other tropical fishes); some in fact barely use anything else. Others find them messy and don't use them at all, but they're worth trying and seeing for yourself.

Apart from the cost, there

is one big problem with feeding frozen foods—sometimes frozen foods get thawed out somewhere along the line between the packer and you, and instead of a package of frozen brine shrimp or bloodworms you get a package of refrozen gray glop that was once frozen brine shrimp or bloodworms. Thawed out and refrozen food is worse than worthless, it's prospectively harmful, and you must be careful. Check the frozen food by dipping a small chunk of it in water to see what happens; if the animals that form the basis of the food stay in individual units (whole) as they drop from the chunk, they should be all right, but if the chunk dissolves as a sort of amorphous gray mass of juices and animal pieces rather than completely whole animals, watch out.

*Many freeze-dried foods are rich in carotenes.*

## Freeze-Dried Foods

Some organisms are best stored when they go through a process known as freeze drying. These organisms are preserved whole, in their original configuration, and with nearly all of their essential nutrients intact. However, such foods can be expensive compared with their frozen counterparts. Nearly all foods offered as "freeze-dried" are also offered as live, fresh, and frozen, so you do have other options should you find that freeze-dried foods are too expensive to utilize.

Freeze-dried shrimp are often used for feeding oscars.

Krill, one type of food that oscars relish and which is not offered alive, is somewhat regularly offered as frozen, and very commonly offered as freeze-dried as well. Krill are small shrimp-like creatures that inhabit the cold sub-Arctic and -Antarctic waters of both the Northern and Southern Hemispheres. They are rich in nutrients and provide outstanding color-enhancing characteristics with their potent alpha- and beta-carotenes. Feeding a wide variety of foods to your oscar is always the best choice. If you have freezers available, perhaps you should opt to use more of the frozen foods, but if not, don't be discouraged. As with most things, each type of food has its loyal supporters, but in the end, variety is the key.

## Non-Commercial Foods

Foods that are not offered on a commercial level are generally referred to as non-commercial foods. This designation is most commonly used when referring to foods that are prepared by the hobbyist himself. Of course, a non-commercial food can be made up of several commercial foods, as they simply act as an ingredient at that point.

## Homemade Foods

If you are the adventurous type and enjoy cooking or food preparation, feel free to experiment with the endless possibilities of formulating your own oscar food. Depending on just how far

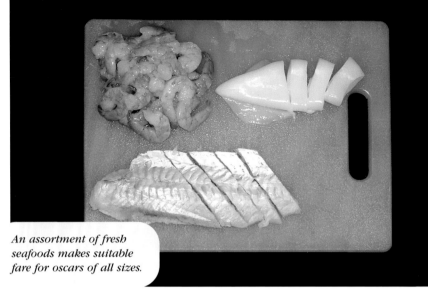

An assortment of fresh seafoods makes suitable fare for oscars of all sizes.

you want to take this endeavor and how much time you have to spend doing so, such a practice can be perhaps the most rewarding experience next to breeding oscars. You can be proud of knowing that you are providing a meal for your oscar(s), one you created out of your own research and understanding of fish nutrition.

To get started, you will need a blending tool (blender, grinder, chopper), the raw ingredients, a binding agent such as a gelatin-based binder, and vitamins or supplements to give your homemade food some nutritive kick.

Your raw ingredients can come from many sources. When possible, it is probably best to use organisms like squid, clams, shrimp, and other seafoods. These are generally going to give you the most value for your dollar

## Spice Things Up

Plainly said, oscars get bored with their food. To spice things up for them, always try new foods, even different brands of the same types of foods. For example, if you're cruising the isles of your local pet shop searching for a new dog bone or cat toy, then pick up a new type of food for your oscar. There are many types of pellets, tablets, wafers, and other forms of food that will do nothing more than offering your oscar something different to eat while adding a new selection of nutrients—what could be better?

in terms of nutritional value and they add a taste that oscars cannot resist. The vitamins and any supplements you choose to add can come from a veterinarian or from an aquaculture supply house. In some instances they can be found at your local grocery store, but check with a board-certified veterinarian who specializes in fish medicine or an aquaculturist for the best places to obtain these additives. Mix the contents together and strain to preferred size, if possible. This can be done with cheesecloth or strainers of various sizes that are available in food stores. Different-sized bits are good for different-sized oscars.

The mash can then be fed immediately to small oscars, or if you prepare this mixture in bulk, you should freeze the remaining portions either in cubes or small packets for later use. Some hobbyists prefer to dry their mixtures out while others prefer to make small pellets or "meatballs" out of them. Whatever you do, make sure the mixture stays as fresh as possible, and do not add too large of a quantity to your aquarium at any one time.

## Live Foods

In most cases, offering live foods to your fishes is the best way to supply them with a broad range of useful nutrients and vitamins. However, live foods can also be the highway for transmittable diseases, so proper precautions should always be taken to ensure that they are fresh and disease-free before offering them to your fishes.

## Live Fishes

In general, oscars prefer to eat live foods whenever possible, and they especially like to eat live fishes. But providing a steady diet of live fishes is an expensive proposition, not to mention a potentially harmful one, too. If you can feed your oscar(s) fishes that you've raised yourself, you can of course keep the cash outlay for food fishes to a minimum, but you'll still have the expense in terms of tank space used to breed or house the

*Live crickets are relished by large oscars.*

*While popular, feeding live feeder fishes to oscars is not the best choice.*

feeder fishes. If you have to constantly buy the feeder fish it can end up costing a lot of money in the long haul, and you'll still have to dedicate a significant amount of tank space to them until they are consumed, because you can't save much unless you buy them in bulk quantities.

In general, live fishes are among the best all-around food for oscars. They are nutritionally sound, easy and usually clean to feed, and almost always available. But there are drawbacks to feeding live fishes. Feeder fishes that have been housed or transported in unsanitary conditions can, and often do, carry parasites and disease-causing organisms that could attack an oscar, and that's a danger that cannot be brushed off. Hobbyists having access to the ocean are fortunate, because the tidal areas along the ocean's shoreline provide a rich diversity of marine life that is suitable oscar fare. Various saltwater and brackish water killifishes of the types that are sold for bait in tackle shops are excellent for oscars. You can even catch your own and have a large supply on hand at any one time. Of course, be sure to check the fish and game laws of the area, as you may need to obtain a fishing license before even dipping a net in the water.

The same applies for other seawater goodies as well. Clams, oysters, shrimps, and to a lesser extent, crabs can all be harvested and utilized as oscar food. Avoid large crabs at all costs as they can potentially kill your oscar with ease. Keep in mind that marine organisms are much more difficult to maintain in good health, and this detracts from their value to a certain extent.

Bodies of fresh water will of course provide many suitable foods for oscars, but fresh-water organisms are much more potentially dangerous regarding the risk of disease transmission compared to marine organisms. Also, the collection of potential oscar food from rivers, lakes, and streams is often regulated by law quite a bit more than with marine habitats, and you really have to be cautious as to what you're collecting.

So, although live fishes are among the best foods to offer oscars, it's not always possible or desirable to provide them as a staple item to oscars. Therefore, most oscar owners have to provide at least some portion of their oscar's diets in non-living form whether they want to or not. Let's not forget that many an oscar has been raised from juvenile to adult without ever eating

### Better Than Fresh

While fresh foods, in most cases, are better than frozen foods, live foods are generally better than fresh. Whenever possible, an offering of live earthworms, feeder fishes, or insects should be given to your oscar(s). In addition to, not in place of, a staple diet of prepared foods, live animals will introduce a spectrum of nutrients that are hard to obtain from anything but live foods.

a living thing (unless a bug or two incidentally fell into the water when the keeper wasn't looking).

49

*Mealworms come in several different sizes, and all make great food for oscars.*

## Insects

Most freshwater fishes consume insects at some point in their lives. Many of these insects are small, flying types that inadvertently land in the water, or in the case of archerfishes they may be shot off low leaves hanging just above the water's surface with a small jet of water. Some fishes, such as the arowanas, are actually accomplished jumpers that are very capable of leaping several feet out of the water in order to capture a beetle or other creepy crawler walking along a leaf or branch above the surface of the water.

Either way, insects are often over-looked as suitable fare for fishes. This is unfortunate, because many species of fishes that are accused of being difficult to keep in captivity will actually do quite well if they are offered something that they actually recognize as food—bugs!

In Nature, oscars feed on a wide variety of foods. However, their favorite food is insects, and since insects are numerous in the tropics of South America, the oscars can choose from quite a selection. Oscars from various regions show remarkable color differences. While coloration depends on more than just diet alone, diet does play a crucial role in determining the

overall intensity of their coloration and pattern.

For example, it is generally believed that insects are responsible for the intense red coloration of oscars and many other cichlids in the Rio Negro, in Brazil. The Rio Negro is a nutrient-poor, blackwater system that feeds into the Amazon River from the northern rainforest. Therefore, attributing this intense coloration to the presence of a mineral or some other nutrient is not possible, so we believe that such coloration is directly related to the fish's diet.

Of all the various species of insects that are available, hobbyists really only need to be familiar with a few. To

*The Expert Knows*

## Oscars Love Bugs!

Insects of all types are relished by oscars, and the broad range of nutrients they offer makes them a natural addition to the diet of oscars in aquariums, too. Pet shops often carry several types of insects, which are more commonly used to feed reptiles and amphibians, but they will generally work very well for oscars. Of these, waxworms, crickets, and mealworms are probably the most commonly found and all of them should be rotated into the staple diet of your oscar.

## Lock Up the Food

**Because oscars are such gluttons, and children love to feed fish, it's wise to keep the fish food out of reach of young children. They may be tempted to feed the oscar, and feed him some more, and more, and before you know it the tank is a smelly mess and the oscar is not as happy as one would think. Having control of the oscar's food is a good way to teach children the responsible way to feed not only a fish, but all pets in general.**

and not collected out behind the woodpile. Pesticides and other pollutants can build up in your fish's internal organs and cause major problems that will dramatically shorten the life of your fish.

The best insects to feed most tropical aquariums fishes are probably mealworms, waxworms, and soft-shelled crickets. There are two major hurdles to overcome when feeding these organisms to your fishes—the size of the insect and their tendancy to block the intestines of your fish. Obviously, a small fish cannot eat a cricket that is nearly the same size as it is, so you have to be prepared with alternatives. One alternative is pellet or flake food that has been formulated with insects or earthworms.

Many medium- and large-sized oscars will accept commercially available insects quite readily. These insects should be offered only a few times a week, since they are extremely high in protein and fat. They can really

51

ensure that you will not add any potentially harmful chemicals to your aquarium, all insects should be purchased through your local pet shop

## Don't Be a Pushover

Before you know it, your new oscar will begin to associate you with their favorite thing on Earth—food! They will be the first to greet you upon walking within sight of their aquarium and may even start to splash water out of the tank in anticipation of being fed. However, don't be a pushover. They should not be fed every time you walk by their aquarium and if they are, then it'll only make a bad situation worse. Develop a feeding regimen and stick to it. Both you and your oscar will be better for it.

cause fish to pack on the weight, especially those fishes that do not have a lot of swimming room in which to work off the calories. Whenever you feed insects to your fishes, you of course have to make every attempt to match them up with food that is the right size.

Live earthworms are one of the best oscar foods out there.

If you have been feeding large amounts of insects to your fish, you may notice that waste is not passing very readily. This would be evidenced by a slight bulge in the body cavity just above the vent. Usually, this blockage is the result of feeding too much of one thing. This happens a little more regularly when feeding with insects due to their hard chitinous exo-skeletons and their tendency to get stuck in the fishes' gut.

Sometimes pet shops will be out of stock on certain live insects. In that case, you may want to try your local bait and tackle shop. They often carry a wide assortment of live insects, especially waxworms, which are great for trout and sunfishes, and often have plenty in stock. Due to their popularity as bait, tackle shops often get regular deliveries of waxworms, so they are usually very fresh.

## Earthwoms

Earthworms have been popular as food for oscars for many years. They are perhaps the best source of safe-to-feed animal protein for many medium and large oscars, and they can certainly be chopped up or minced for feeding to smaller oscars.

Earthworms are soft-bodied and therefore do not have the chance to build up in the fish's gut like animals having a hard chitinous skeleton. They are digested rather quickly, and their nutrients are able to be processed quickly, too. Fishes that consume large numbers of worms on a regular basis are usually quite chunky. Such an observation leads to the conclusion that earthworms are high in fat as well.

Feeding only a small number of worms to your fishes daily, or even every other day or every third day, would help to lessen the possibility of obesity. Always being cautious about feeding techniques is one practice that will prove invaluable in the future. In many cases, it is better to underfeed than to overfeed.

Obtaining earthworms is fairly simple. First, nearly every bait and tackle shop in existence carries them and often in different sizes and quantities. Also, many retail fish shops carry them as well. This is especially

true with full-line pet shops that may also carry birds, small animals, and fishes since earthworms make a good food source for those animals, too.

If you wish to collect your own earthworms, doing so is quite simple. The first place to look is in a compost pile or another area that contains high-nutrient soil and dirt. Of course, gardens work well, too. You can also look under partially rotten wood or under slabs of rock that may be covering soil. Simply take a small shovel and turn over the soil slowly and methodically. You will often see the worms trying to "worm" their way back under it.

On warm days, you may need to dig a bit deeper than on cool days. Earthworms never like the heat, and if you have purchased them before at any of the above mentioned shops, you will

*Ghost/grass shrimp are good treats for oscars, but their relatively high price makes them impractical for frequent use.*

notice that they should have removed them from a refrigerator. Early fall and spring seem to be the best times of the year to collect these animals. Be creative in your collecting techniques but always be certain to get them from areas that are not likely to have high levels of contaminants.

## Other Live Foods

Besides the live foods that are customarily obtained from tropical fish stores, there are a number of other live foods that oscars will readily eat. Some of them are easy to obtain, whereas others are hard to get. Some are easy to get in some places but hard to get in other places. Take live crayfish (crawfish) for example. They are excellent food for big oscars and are obtainable in good numbers in many parts of the United States and other countries. But they are not available everywhere, even in countries where they exist in Nature, so not everyone can use them even though they may wish to.

Aquarium snails are another interesting, and formerly popular, food for oscars. They are an excellent food for oscars, by the way, and should probably be used more than they are. Red ramshorn snails seem to be especially useful and you can keep a culture of them going in a small aquarium and just drop a few crushed ones into your oscar aquarium from time to time.

## How Much & How Often to Feed

Oscars are gluttons and they will eat until they become sick. Of course, that would be bad, so you have to draw the line at some point. Unfortunately there is no widely accepted rule of thumb or standards for feeding oscars. All that can be presented here is a guide based on years, and years, and some more years of

*Aquarium snails are an excellent addition to an Oscars diet.*

*Oscars quickly become accomplished beggars.*

keeping oscars of all types and sizes. In general, small oscars (under 4 in. [10 cm] TL) should be fed three times daily and only the amount of food that will be needed to slightly round off their bellies. Smaller oscars should be fed more than larger oscars because their growth rate is higher and they need the extra nutrition compared to medium and larger oscars, whose growth rates have already slowed. Medium oscars (from 4 in. [10 cm] to 8 in. [20 cm] TL) should also be fed daily, but only one or two offerings of food should be given, and again only the amount needed to slightly round

off the fish's belly. Adult oscars (from 8 in. [20 cm] and up) don't need to eat daily but can certainly be fed a small feeder fish, live cricket or earthworm, or a few pellets each day with larger feedings offered three time weekly. Due to the actual size of adult oscars, it's often hard to tell just how much food is needed in order to satisfy them, which by the way the terms "satisfy" and "oscar" should really not be used in the same sentence. But at least you can satisfy his nutritional needs even if you can never satisfy his psychological cravings.

# Chapter 4

# Feeling Good

Just like every other aquarium fish, oscars sometimes come down with an illness that needs to first be identified and then treated appropriately. Of course, there are some pathogens that are much more commonly encountered than others and these are usually easier to treat, since medications are generally available from a variety of sources. In addition to illness, oscars are prone to injuries, which is mainly due to their large size and inquisitive manner.

They are sort of like trouble-makers in the sense that if there is a possibility of getting into something that they shouldn't then they'll usually find a way to do so. More often than not, such trouble leads to an injury.

## Injuries

There are a whole host of injuries that can affect oscars, and other fishes, too. Fighting, pre-spawning behavior, and tank re-arranging are just a few things that can cause such problems. Since oscars are inquisitive beasts, they often try to move things that really should not be touched. For example, heaters, thermometers, filter intake tubes, filter return nozzles, and even covers are not out of an oscar's realm for taste-testing. Be aware that injuries can lead to bacterial infections, which may lead to

other complications down the road. Keeping the aquarium's water clean is the best way to prevent any injuries from turning deadlier than they are by themselves.

## Illnesses

Oscars are less susceptible to some illnesses than other aquarium fishes and more susceptible to others. In the case of those illnesses to which they are more susceptible, the heightened susceptibility usually is the result of the oscar's size or pugnacious nature. The growth of the fungus *Saprolegnia* on untreated wounds caused by fighting is an example. Small, comparatively peaceful schooling fishes such as neon tetras and zebra danios suffer from fungus invasions much less frequently than oscars, mostly because they are much less likely to sustain wounds

*This tiger oscar is showing some wounds from a fight. With proper care, he will heal up in a few days.*

irritant to the fish, and it's relatively easy to cure. Now make no mistake about it, if the aquarium conditions are such where an ick outbreak manifests into an all-out infestation then ick is surely capable of destroying even the hardiest of fishes—including oscars.

when maintained with their own kind, yet oscars are much less frequently infested with the dinoflagellate *Oodinium* than, say, bettas or killies seem to be.

## Ick

The most common illness of aquarium fishes is a protozoan parasite affectionately referred to as "ick," or sometimes even "ich." This disease organism causes an outbreak of a rash of tiny white, salt-like spots all over the body and fins of the affected fish. The white spots are not the actual disease organism itself but are the cysts in which the protozoans live prior to adopting a free-swimming phase and actively seeking a host fish. There are two good things about ick: it's generally not a quick killing protozoan, being more of an

Ick outbreaks are usually, but not always, initiated by an abrupt drop in the aquarium's temperature or by exposing the fish to others that are infected with the parasite. Ick is highly transmissible, and if one fish in a tank has it then it can easily spread to its tankmates if the infected fish isn't moved to a quarantine tank to heal. The best way to actually cure any fish having ick is to ask your local pet shop for a suitable medication. There are many types on the market and all of them work to one extent or the next. A word of warning though, any medication that contains dyes may stain the aquarium's sealant and other things (i.e., rocks, bogwood, etc.) that it comes in contact with. Regardless, there are a number of products that when used properly will clear a tank of the parasites. Always consult with a professional before treating any fish, however, as there are hidden dangers.

## Velvet

Parasites of the genera *Oodinium and Amyloodinium* are generally referred to as "velvet" disease because of the

SMALL FRY

## Teaching Respect for Living Things

All living things deserve to be respected. This applies to oscars in the sense that by providing them with good water, good food, and a good setup it can then be said that the oscar's needs are being respected. Other points to consider with regards to respect for oscars is the fact that they don't particularly like being teased or taunted. Don't smack their aquarium's glass, don't offer food then scoop it up, and most importantly don't allow their aquariums to become a cesspool of dirt and filth. A nicely set up oscar aquarium with good water quality and healthy fish is the goal that all oscar keepers should be striving for.

velvety appearance the fish take on when they're infected with them. Velvet is more stubborn to cure than ick, but there are many types of effective medications that will clear a tank of these protozoa, too. The best cure for this problem is prevention through water changes and cleanliness.

## Bacterial & Fungal Infections

There are many species of bacteria and fungi that can infect oscars. Most of these take hold on wounds that the oscar suffered from fighting with tankmates or some other form of battle. Both bacterial and fungal infections can become dangerous but treating them is significantly more problematic than identifying them because some medications are so strong that they themselves can kill your fishes, either directly or indirectly. One of the biggest concerns when treating an oscar that has a bacterial infection specifically is also killing off the good bacteria in the tank. You see,

*Juvenile oscars seem to be especially prone to parasitic infections.*

antibiotics are indiscriminant as to which bacteria they kill. They destroy both good and bad bacteria equally. Don't forget that good bacteria are responsible for maintaining a balance in your aquarium and if it dies off then your aquarium will go off-balance in a relatively short period of time.

As with velvet, the best way to cure bacterial and fungal infections is to prevent them from happening in the first place. To do this, simply perform regular partial water changes, keep your filters clean and functioning properly, and don't overfeed. It's all really simple in the end.

### Viral Infections

These little critters are another story entirely and their treatment is beyond the scope of this book. Generally, a virus of the genus *Lymphocystis* is the only type that hobbyists come in contact with on a regular basis but there are certainly plenty of others. *Lymphocystis*, also referred to as "lymph," is easily identified by the whitish cauliflower-like growths that grow from the fins and scales of the fish. Oscars rarely get this disease and even rarer is it fatal. Usually, the growths just fall off after a long time—sometimes it takes a year for this to happen.

The Expert Knows

### The Excercise Factor

Oscars can often be seen just lying about the tank. This can, at times, cause their keepers great concern. The water tests out fine, you just cleaned the tank last week, he ate like a pig yesterday and so on but today he is just sitting there. What's wrong? Probably nothing. Oscars are lazy creatures and after a while, believe it or not, your oscar may just begin sitting around.

### Indigestion

Although it can't be classified as a disease or put down as an infestation by parasites, indigestion happens to be something that oscars are occasionally troubled with, and usually for the same reason that people are—overeating! Oscars are gluttons and will keep on eating as long as their keepers keep on giving them food; again, like people, they don't always get away with it. An oscar with indigestion shows his indisposition by sulking and refusing to eat; a fish so affected also sometimes shows peculiar body orientation in the water, standing still or swimming with his head down. The latter movement is often accompanied by a slight cant to

the body so that
the fish is not
perfectly vertical
in the water.
Sometimes an oscar
with indigestion will
do barrel-rolls throughout the tank,
and sometimes it will even give out
a good approximation of a human
burp. The best cure for indigestion
is to leave the fish without food for
at least a few days, preferably one
week. This allows the fish's digestive
system to readjust itself and come to
a proper balance.

*Some oscars appear hunch-backed. This can be a genetic abnormality.*

Once feeding is to resume, only offer
small amounts of small foods. Some
people even try to feed their oscars
peas, and if they eat them then great.

### Recognizing Symptons

Oscars by and large are resistant to
many illnesses. However, being that
they're fish they can and do come
down with diseases once in a while.
Regardless of what disease or illness an
oscar gets they generally show similar
signs of distress. Just as with
indigestion, oscars usually sulk and may
even retire to the bottom of their
aquarium when they are feeling blue.
Many fishes, oscars included, will go
off-feed almost immediately upon
coming down with a sickness. The best
thing that you can do for your oscar, in
addition to water changes, is on a daily
basis simply watch him swim around
and be an oscar. Once you have
developed this connection with him,
it's easy to tell when he's not feeling
well by the actions and body language
that he'll exhibit.

### Disease Prevention & Treatment

Although the treatment of some
diseases have already been touched on,
it's important to focus on a few factors
that are very important in treating sick
fishes. The most important thing to
keep in mind when keeping fish is to
keep them healthy and to do this you
should focus your efforts on preventing
diseases and problems from happening
in the first place. Hobbyists should not
have to medicate their aquariums on a
regular basis, but they should have a
basic understanding of how to
recognize a disease and when to get
some medication for a sick fish. To do

this, you don't have to be a veterinarian but you should have someone to consult with.

Pet shops, aquarium wholesalers, local veterinarians, public aquariums, and research institutions usually have a professional on staff who is knowledgeable in the treatment of fish diseases. But before you treat a disease you must identify it, and identify it properly. This in and of itself is very problematic and beginners or even experienced hobbyists are not advised to treat anything unless it has been positively identified and approved by a professional.

If, and when, your fish gets sick and you find out exactly what type of problem it has be sure to use any medications that are required to treat the problem strictly as to how the manufacturer advises. Any variation on this and you could turn one potential problem (the sick fish) into another problem entirely (a dead fish). This all being said, if you feel that your oscar is sick consult a local professional for the proper methods in which to treat the problem.

The best way to keep oscars healthy is to avoid excess in all forms, whether in temperature range, amount and type of food offered, or water quality. Don't chill or overheat the fish, don't over-feed the fish, don't

## Using Salt

Salt has been used, both as a general tonic and a disease treatment, in aquariums for decades. Is it really necessary? Does it really do anything? The answers to both questions are yes and no. Salt is needed by fishes for stability on the cellular level. That is, they will be thrown fatally out of balance should there be an absence of salt in their water. On the other hand, too much salt will do just the opposite, but with the same consequence—death.

However, salt has been known to assist a freshwater fish in ridding itself of external parasites. So adding a little bit of salt to an oscar aquarium is a good thing because it will help the oscar to keep parasites off of them, right? Well, mostly yes but not always. Parasites are adaptive little creatures and they quickly become salt-tolerant. Basically, this back and forth can go on forever about salt.

The best, and safest, recommendation about using salt in any freshwater aquarium is to consult a local professional and never use more than the manufacture advises. One thing to keep in mind about salt is that salt doesn't evaporate and if it's added over and over again it will surely have a negative effect on your oscar's health.

# Ten Tips to Proper Quarantine

**5** Keep the quarantine aquarium covered at all times, new oscars may try to jump out and a sturdy cover will keep them in.

**6** Remove any uneaten food at once. If the oscar hasn't eaten all of the food that you offered him within a 5-minute period then you've overfed him. Remove the uneaten food and adjust the amount you are offering him.

The importance of quarantining a newly acquired oscar cannot be underestimated. The following quick tips will help you to do it right and best of all it will make the process more fun and enjoyable for both you and the fish!

**7** Perform frequent partial water changes on all quarantine aquariums. This will help ensure a more balanced, stable environment.

**1** Keep a quarantine aquarium warm; preferably around 82°F (27°C) and check the temperature often in case of heater malfunction.

**8** Use an airpump to add extra oxygen to the quarantine aquarium's water—especially if you are medicating him, as medication sometimes makes it harder for the fish to breathe.

**2** Cover the back, bottom, and sides of a quarantine aquarium with a dark background or paint. This will help the new oscar feel more comfortable.

**9** Keep the water level in a quarantine aquarium lower than that of a display aquarium. This will allow better gas transfer at the water's surface.

**3** Feed your new oscar small meals on a frequent basis, and try different foods. The more foods that he will eat the healthier he will be.

**10** Never medicate with more than one medication at a time unless directed to do so by the advice of certified professional. Multiple medications may cancel the effectiveness of one or more medications or worse still, may create a toxic compound and further harm your oscar.

**4** Don't quarantine more than one oscar at a time unless the quarantine aquarium is very large, say more than 50 gallons (189 l) in volume.

subject the fish to contamination by exposing it to a sick fish, don't crowd the fish, don't let pollutants build up in their tanks, and you should have very few disease problems to deal with. Treat oscars well and they'll reward you with years and years of entertainment and fascination and even a fishy sort of reciprocal affection, and perhaps also a few thousand baby oscars; treat them badly and they'll only give you the same kind of grief you give them.

## Quarantine Your Oscar!

Whenever possible, quarantine any new fish before placing them into a display aquarium. This will help ensure that any diseases or disorders will become apparent before it's too late and other fishes have been subjected to the infected oscar.

Quarantine aquariums don't have to be extensive and in fact it's better if they're not. For most oscars, a 20-gallon (75 l) aquarium will suffice for an average quarantine period, which is usually 21 days long. Even really large oscars can live for a little while in a small aquarium.

The quarantine aquarium's decor should be very sparse or nothing at all. This is mainly due to problems with medicating and aquarium decor's ability to absorb the medication like a sponge. Additionally, decor is expensive and there is little need to set up two fully outfitted aquariums when one is simply going to be empty in a brief period of time. Also, quarantining should not be a hassle. It should be able to be done in a simple, in-expensive, and effective manner.

An average quarantine aquarium should consist of the following: the tank and stand, a cover (lighting optional), a seasoned sponge filter or power filter without a chemical filtrant, heater and thermometer, and maybe a rock or piece of PVC pipe for the oscar to hide behind. Of course, you can make them a little more dramatic, such as by adding inert rock structures and the like but as mentioned, that's not really necessary.

65

Feeling Good

# Chapter 5

# Getting Along

One of the biggest hurdles hobbyists face is the compatibility of the fishes they choose to keep in their aquariums, and this is a big issue with oscars as well. Oscars by and large are loners, although pairs will form and stay together for one mating at least. It's unknown if oscars will pair bond for life in Nature or not.

O scars are generally not social among themselves or other fishes, unless a small group of oscars is maintained in a very large aquarium where limited schooling behavior among other oscars is sometimes witnessed. Due to this antisocial tendency, they also tend to be unpredictable when kept with other, non-related fishes. When it comes to the topic of an oscar's compatibility with other oscars and even with other fishes for that matter, only some brief guidelines can be offered that hopefully will make your choices in tankmate selection the right ones.

## Choosing Compatible Tankmates

First and foremost, it has to be stressed once again that oscars are highly unpredictable creatures. They can bully any fish too large to eat or befriend a feeder goldfish intended to serve as an appetizer. There really is no rhyme or reason to their behavior towards other fishes. Of course, most oscars see anything small enough to fit in their mouths as food, but even still, you'd be surprised at just how many hobbyists have reported that their oscars selected one or two from a few dozen feeder goldfish to befriend and allowed the goldfish to mingle in the tank. Often, such instances result in the goldfish actually growing to the same size as the oscar over time.

While oscars may play lord of their domain, they can just as easily be lorded over. Other large fishes, like some cichlids, sunfishes, basses, and other tankbusters can easily turn the tables on an oscar—even a big one—and before you know it, the oscar is the one that is cowering in the corner with ragged fins and missing scales. Of course, what you really want is a tank where all your fishes just get along, right?

Well, that is a difficult feat, but it can be done as long as you have a basic

*This albino oscar is sharing his home with a large silver arowana.*

## Some Good Choices for the Oscar Tank

The following fishes represent a small fraction of suitable tankmates for most oscars. Remember, each oscar has its own personality and must be watched carefully with other fishes.

1. Banded leporinus
2. Striped leporinus
3. Threespot leporinus
4. Black lancer catfish
5. Pumpkinseed sunfish
6. Spotted metynnis
7. Redhook silver dollar
8. Butterfly peacock cichlid
9. Chameleon cichlid
10. Red hump eartheater
11. Severums
12. Chocolate cichlids
13. Jeweled eartheaters
14. Clown loach
15. Tinfoil barb

....and many, many more!

understanding of the needs of the fish you intend to keep. This is the principal reason for why you should always research a particular species prior to actually obtaining it.

## A Step-By-Step Approach

The first thing you should do when selecting fishes to serve as tankmates for your oscar is to make a list of the fishes that interest you. Look through various aquarium-related material, both in print and on the Internet, and make a list of the fishes that you like. Whenever possible, list both the trade (common) name(s) as well as the scientific name, if available.

After you have drawn up your list of names, you can begin to research each fish species independently. Be as thorough as possible; talk to other oscar keepers (both past and present), pet shop employees, and anyone else whom you think can help you in finding out as much as possible about the fishes on your list. Web-based forums where you can interact with other hobbyists are always a great place to do this, too. This research is not just about what you can and cannot keep with your oscar but it's about researching fishes in general. And much of what you learn will help you down the road in future fishkeeping endeavors.

Next, cross check the needs of your oscar with the needs of the fishes that you've selected. More than likely, the vast majority of them will not be compatible with oscars, but some probably will be. Be sure to pay particularly close attention to certain major concerns such as tank-size requirements, feeding preferences, and overall aggression tendencies in the fish. Those species that match closely should be placed on a new, separate list.

Now you should have two lists: one with a bunch of crosses through it to delete incompatible species and one with some semi-finalists. Take this list to whatever resources you trust the most. They can be a pet shop employee, a coworker with many years of experience keeping aquariums, or whoever else fits the bill.

See what input they can offer, and look into any related species they suggest and which may not be on your list. For example, you may have come across the triangle cichlid, also known as the waroo, (*Uaru amphiacanthoides*) in your travels and placed it on your list. As you probably found out, this species is suitable for inclusion with oscars. However, the waroo has a close cousin, the long-finned waroo, that is also acceptable to house with oscars of a similar size. The same can be said for non-cichlid species such as the silver dollar *(Metynnis hypsauchen)*, which is very common and perfectly suitable to keep with oscars as long as the silver dollars are larger than the oscars. But you would be less likely to come across the blackband silver dollar (*Myleus schomburgkii*) even though they are just as suitable to keep with oscars as their cousins.

*Oscars are very competitive with other fishes for food.*

*Eels are best avoided for inclusion in the oscar aquarium.*

## Fish to Avoid

There is little doubt that the vast majority of the fishes that you'll come across are actually not suitable to house with oscars, well at least not in normal home aquariums, and you may be surprised as to why they're not compatible. Fishes can be too small or too large, too aggressive or not aggressive enough; they can also have vastly different feeding habits. This section provides a brief summary of the fishes that should be avoided without question. They are generally best avoided because of their size and the type of care they need but there are other reasons, too. Read carefully!

## African Tigerfishes

These behemoths are native to large bodies of water in Africa. They are fast, voracious predators that grow more than 3 ft. (100 cm) in length and need huge aquariums to accommodate them. African tigerfishes are generally too aggressive to keep with oscars and are best left to public display aquaria.

## Eels

Many species of eels are commonly found in the aquarium trade. Most of these grow to a size that makes them suitable for inclusion in an oscar setup. Unfortunately, they have a nasty habit that they simply cannot be broken of—they are able to slither out of nearly every aquarium that they're placed in. They should be avoided for this reason,

## Some Poor Cichlid Choices for the Oscar Aquarium

1. Jack Dempsey cichlid
2. Red devil cichlid
3. Midas cichlid
4. Wolf cichlid
5. Jaguar cichlid
6. Green terrors
7. Texas cichlid
8. Carpinte cichlid
9. Blackbelt cichlid
10. Festae cichlid

Please note that some of the above species will do well with oscars only in very large setups but generally they are not recommended to be housed with them otherwise.

and as if the potential of finding a slimy eel slithering across your floor isn't bad enough, eels tend to attempt their escapes at night when the lights are out, and their busy actions at times frighten oscars to the point where they haphazardly dart around the aquarium. Such behavior almost always leads to injury, which in turn can lead to other health problems.

### Gars

Gars are an unusual group of fishes. They are often tolerant of oscars but they don't react well to the aggressive food snatching behavior that oscars exhibit when feeding time comes around. Often, gars will actually become so frightened that they actually leap from the aquarium, or at the very least they damage themselves while trying. These large-growing primitive fishes are best left to experienced hobbyists who have setups specifically dedicated to keeping them.

### North American Sunfishes

For some reason, hobbyists will often try to house their oscars with the freshwater sunfishes of the family Centrarchidae. Occasionally this will work while other times it will not. It's best to

only attempt this with large oscars housed in large aquariums, as most sunfishes grow to almost 1 ft. (30 cm)!

### Pacu

Pacu are huge-growing fishes that make very convenient tankmates for oscars. In fact, they are almost the perfect tankmate for them—if only they didn't grow to 40 in. (100 cm). These omnivores enjoy munching on grapes as much as they do shrimp. With their almost human-like dentition, they can easily crack many types of nuts that fall into their watery domain. As juveniles, Pacu are attractively colored, but as they grow they tend to fade to a black and silvery colored fish.

### Pimelodids

These long-whiskered catfishes are

mostly suitable, with some exceptions. Three of these are the red-tailed catfish (*Phractocephalus hemioliopterus*) and the tiger shovel-nose catfishes (*Pseudoplatystoma fasciatum* & *P. tigrinum*). All three of these species attain an adult length of over 3 ft. (100 cm) and are totally unsuitable for the oscar aquarium. In fact, they are almost completely un-suitable for nearly all home aquariums.

Basically, an oscar is an appetizer for an adult red-tailed catfish or tiger shovelnose.

## Piranhas

While the aggressive, man-eating nature of piranhas is almost a complete myth, these big, toothy tetras are actually ruthless on oscars. With their large paddle-like fins and bulky bodies, oscars make tempting treats to the carnivorous piranhas.

## Multilevel Stocking

Once you have determined just what species, and how many of them, you're going to add to your oscar aquarium you can break them down one step further. The area of the aquarium that they occupy can be closely paid attention to. By adding fish that inhabit the bottom-, mid-, and upper-water areas you'll make for a more pleasing and naturally accurate aquarium overall.

## Snakeheads

Not only do these fishes grow to monstrous proportions but they are illegal to own in many states and completely illegal to import into the United States. Hobbyists in Canada and other nations can still get them, but regardless of their availability, some species like the popular red snakehead (Channa micropeltes) grow to a size where they could easily swallow even an adult oscar. Aside from their massive size, snakeheads are actually pretty

calm and many hobbyists report that they will defend fellow tankmates from new additions that may be overly aggressive.

## Wolf Fishes

Basically looking like baseball bats with a large set of teeth, wolf fishes are very aggressive and can inflict a lot of damage to your oscar. Some species grow very large but most specimens are no larger than 12" (30 cm). These fishes are best left to those who will afford them with a tank all their own.

## Wyckii Catfish

The wyckii catfish is probably the most aggressive catfish that can be kept in home aquariums. They are basically

This oscar pond is home to more than a dozen adult albino oscars in total.

Oscars

intolerant of any other fish housed with them. It's not uncommon for hobbyists to report that their wyckii catfish have become very tame and would even approach the glass when people came in the same room that the fish was kept in. Strangely, one hobbyist reported that his would only rise to the surface when he approached the aquarium but when others did it would not pay any attention to them.

## Other Fishes

Of course, the aforementioned fishes are really just the tip of the iceberg when it comes to species that are unsuitable, or mostly unsuitable, for inclusion in aquariums where the primary species to be displayed is an oscar. If you notice, one group of fishes that is suspiciously missing is those from the family Cichlidae—the oscar's family! Why?

## A Fish-Eat-Fish World

Oscars will consume any fish that is small enough to fit in their large mouths. It's very important to realize that what you may consider a safe fish and what the oscar may consider a safe fish are two different things. Oscars are gluttons, and animals that eat like oscars often have eyes bigger than their stomachs!

Well, there are too many to list. It's important to note that just because oscars are cichlids it doesn't mean that all cichlids can be successfully kept together.

## Stocking & Overstocking

The most common compatibility issue with any aquarium arises from overstocking or overcrowding your

### SMALL FRY

### Explaining Fish Compatability

Children love to pick out their own fish, and they often think that any fish can be kept together. When children are allowed to pick out there own fish they should be given choices based on previous research done by the parents so that regardless of what species is picked, it will work. Of course, nothing is ever guaranteed and a fish that is supposed to work usually will, but living animals don't always do what they are supposed to. Regardless, issues as such should be explained to kids from the beginning so they will be less upset, and hopefully more interested in why things didn't work out the way they were supposed to.

aquarium. And often, to make matters worse, the information on how many of a certain type of fish to include in your oscar aquarium may be based on the assumption that you will be using adequate filtration and making frequent large-scale water changes. Of course, you should be using adequate filtration and making frequent large-scale water changes!

When keeping large species, like oscars, you will basically have to come up with your own stocking schemes but remember that it is the total body mass of the fish that determines how much bioload that fish actually puts on a system. Four 3-inch (7.5-centimeter) juvenile oscars will be nowhere near the total mass of one 12-inch (30 cm) adult oscar.

# Chapter 6

# Who Am I?

Oscars are available in a stunning array of selectively bred strains. Some of these are offshoots of the red oscar, like the gold, sunshine, and lemon strains to name a just few, but many are strains of the tiger oscar, too. However, in the end, no matter what the strain, they can all be traced back to the original, wild-type *Astronotus ocellatus*, which was the only strain that was available many years ago.

## It's Your Choice!

Some hobbyists love all types of oscars while others can't stand anything that's not natural. It's your choice really, but it's important that you realize that each oscar strain is basically the same as the next when it comes to their care and husbandry in aquariums. On that note, it should also be mentioned, however, that not all oscars will grow to the size of the wild-type oscars. Albino, leucistic, red, and snow oscars specifically don't grow much over 12 inches (30 cm) on average. And while they are capable of growing to 16 inches (40 cm) or more, tiger oscars usually don't get much over 14 inches (35 cm) TL. In the end though, an oscar is still a good deal thicker than most other aquarium fishes so just because you intend to keep only one or two albino oscars

doesn't mean that you can get away with any smaller of a tank than you would need for a couple of tiger oscars.

## Oscar Segregation

Previously mentioned was an interesting note reported by some hobbyists who have kept multiple strains of oscars together. These hobbyists note that when multiple specimens of different oscar strains are housed in the same aquarium they tend to stay more closely associated with the members of their strain, but when single specimens of multiple strains are housed together they will interact with each other as if they were blind to the colors of each individual oscar. This behavior is not actually unique in fishes but is rather unique among oscars,

*These juvenile oscars were wild collected from the Rio Negro, Brazil.*

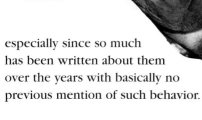

*A common oscar, the type from which all of the ornamental strains were derived.*

especially since so much has been written about them over the years with basically no previous mention of such behavior.

## Selective Breeding

The variations on the original oscar are astounding, a true testimony to what can be accomplished through a rather simple concept called selective breeding. In a nutshell, selective breeding is the removal of young from a brood which show a desired trait to raise them in isolation to adulthood to spawn against either their parents or other specimens which share the selected trait. Selective breeding is the same method that guppy and betta breeders have used for decades and that Japanese koi breeders have used for centuries. The Far East seems to be the leaders in selective breeding techniques, and it should be no surprise that breeders in Singapore, Thailand, and Malaysia are the epicenters for producing strains of several types of cichlids, including oscars.

## The Many Faces of Oscar

The following catalogue provides a brief description of the most popular types of oscar strains and sports

---

## Male or Female, How Can I Tell?

Oscars are downright difficult to accurately sex. They are considered monomorphic, which means they have no visible external sex differences. This makes obtaining a pair of adults very difficult. Some advanced hobbyists, however, use the "vent method" to determine the sex of their oscars. This is also called "venting." The vent method involves the removal of the oscars from their tanks in order to inspect the genital papillae, which is located just posterior to their anus. This method is best left to professionals who have received the proper training to determine the sex of fishes in this manner.

## What Are These Eyespots For?

The eyespots on the base of the tail (caudal) fin are present in almost all strains of oscars, more so on some compared to others. Wild oscars from Peru, and some other localities, have a row of these spots just under their dorsal fins, too. Regardless, the actual usefulness of this interesting pattern is highly controversial. Most agree, however, that the eyespots act as a set of "false eyes" to confuse would-be predators into attacking a less-critical area of their body. Such a pattern gives the oscars a 50/50 chance that the predator will attack the false eyes instead of the real eyes.

available to hobbyists on a regular basis. Since common names are confusing and inaccurate at best, you may know different names for some of the ones mentioned below simply based on their descriptions. If this is true, don't be discouraged, as neither you, the pet shop that carries the oscars, or the information herein is wrong. Rather, it just proves that common names can be vastly different for each type of fish, and this even more true when you're dealing with the comparison of one oscar type from nation to nation. For example, what we know as the common oscar here in the United States may be known as the green oscar in Germany.

### Common/Wild-Type Oscars

The oscar that started it all was the wild oscar, referred to as the common oscar. A brown to green base color with varying amounts of black, red, orange, and cream coloring, these fish are highly variable and gave rise to the many, many different colors that are now offered. Today,

*Adult oscars from the Rio Negro commonly show a lot of red in their undersides.*

*Some wild-type oscars exhibit a lot of green as adults.*

common oscars are still popular but not nearly as much as the tiger, red tiger, red, or albino oscars.

Sometimes, wild-type or common oscars are referred to as "black" oscars, too. This name seems to be especially common in Europe, and is only used occasionally in the United States. Black oscars are not entirely black, but their colors are heavily muted giving them a black and white appearance similar to that of an old black and white film.

Although the wild-type oscar is still popular among hobbyists, and is widely available at aquarium shops, most of these are not wild at all. They have been bred for many generations on fish farms all over the world and in the tanks of dedicated hobbyists. This is an advantage in that the animals are free of disease, and the captive specimens are usually far easier to breed compared to their wild counterparts.

Even though the domesticated oscar is somewhat variable in appearance, most of them don't quite have the richness of coloration that is possessed by the specimens in the wild—although there is quite a bit of variation in the wild specimens, too. Tropical fish collectors as well as ichthyologists report that individuals from the same body of water may exhibit radically different coloration and pattern. For example, one specimen may have three or four dorsal ocelli while another may have none at all. The main constant is that

*Green oscars are just a color morph of the wild-type oscars.*

there is nearly always an eye spot on the base of the tail fin.

Recently, rare fish importers have been bringing in shipments of wild-collected oscars from many different regions in the Amazon basin and many of these look drastically different from the original wild-type oscars. Regardless, it's still fairly easy to identify them as wild-type oscars.

### Chocolate Oscars

Some red oscars never seem to grow out of their intermediate coloring. When this happens, they will usually take on a brown overcast and often they're given the name of chocolate oscars. Is it a sales pitch? Probably so.

### Gold/Bronze Oscars

Essentially, the gold oscar is a dull-colored red oscar, but not to be confused with a poor-colored red oscar, which is generally more pinkish rather than red. Some hobbyists like this type of subdued coloration and therefore it is still found, even after decades since its introduction from fish farmers in Asia. The bronze oscar is basically just a darker gold oscar.

### Green Oscars

This name has been attached to wild-type or common oscars that simply exhibit more green. Some have speculated that certain oscars from different localities in the Amazon basin show more green compared to others but such specific information has not been made available with any type of authority. Also, very old adult oscars of both the tiger and wild-type strains often show more green than do younger fish.

## Lemon Oscars

A new arrival on the oscar scene is the lemon oscar. These brilliantly colored yellow and white fish are very striking—especially as mature adults. Some specimens can be as bright as a yellow canary while others can show just a dusting of yellow. This strain is also referred as the lemon-drop oscar, and was developed in Asia.

## Lutino/Leucistic Oscars

Most of the time, an "albino" oscar is not albino at all—it's leucistic (or xanthic). A leucistic animal has no dark pigment, but it can have yellow or red pigment. It usually has red eyes like an albino. A true albino has no pigment at all and appears white with red eyes (since you can see the blood in the unpigmented eye). An unusual trait of oscars is that sometimes a leucistic ani-mal shows sooty coloration on the fins, and sometimes on the body, too. Often this dirty appearance varies over time and is sometimes lost as the animal grows. In practical usage, however, any oscar with a white body rather than a brown one is called an "albino."

## Purple Oscars

There are two types of purple oscars; one type is a red oscar that simply never matured in color from its intermediate stage, and the other is a dyed white oscar, which is essentially the same fish as an albino or snow oscar but has been stripped of its protective slime coating and placed in a strong purple-colored dye. The former has been used to fix this sport into a full strain but has never really caught on so therefore the fish has become pretty rare and are happened upon generally by accident.

Occasionally, if a group of red oscars is raised up together you'll sometimes get a purple oscar mixed in the group, but again this is quite rare. Generally, purple-colored oscars do not, or should not, cost more money than a standard red

*"Albino" oscars that have yellow or red pigmentation are more appropriately referred to as lutino, leucistic or xanthic oscars..*

A beautiful example of a mature red oscar.

oscar of the same size, and the purple dyed oscar will most surely be a dirty white color as an adult because the dye wears off pretty fast.

### Red Oscars

Early in 1969, the aquarium trade started to receive regular shipments of a new oscar strain known as the red oscar. The red oscar was a new and exciting fish, and in the opinion of many it was far better looking compared to the common, or wild-type, oscar and it soon caught on in a big way. Today, red oscars are widely available throughout the hobby and from basically every dealer that carries tropical fish. They were developed by Charoen Pattabongse, a

Red tiger oscars exhibit a lot more red compared to a normal tiger oscar.

Thai businessman, who discovered a few aberrant individuals in a group of regular oscars and eventually developed his find into a viable strain, which breeds true.

Some red oscars have intensely red flanks, these are referred to as "super reds."

## Red Tiger Oscars

Juveniles of this strain appear to closely resemble wild-type oscars of similar size and age. However, as they grow and mature, red tigers develop increased red coloration, mostly on the lower half of the body, which are sometimes referred to as "red-bellied oscars." In some instances, the red coloration will extend far up into the flanks and the fish will exhibit more red than black or brown.

## Tiger Oscars

Probably the most notable strain that originated from the wild-type oscar was the tiger oscar. The tiger oscar is basically the first commercial variant of the oscar and the "improvement" amounts to a selection for more orange or red coloration in the individuals, while retaining all the other colors. These artificial varieties are started

*Tiger oscars are probably the most common of all the types of oscars available.*

when an individual specimen shows a qualitative difference from other fish. The fish is bred, and the custom has been, with livebearers for example, to breed the progeny back to the original variant or "sport." However, since oscars take a long time to mature, and often mate for life in aquariums, this normal procedure is more difficult to follow with them. It is probably for that reason that there are not more color varieties of oscars. Occasionally, the name "snakeskin" is used to describe tiger oscars that have a unique, snakeskin-like pattern on their flanks.

*Here is a nice albino red oscar.*

## Albino Oscars

Albino oscars were developed long (about twenty years) after the red oscar and its variations were developed, but only a few years after the development of the veil tailed oscars. Over the years, they

have attained certain popularity, although it has lagged behind that of the tiger and red oscar strains, not to mention the wild, unspoiled strain. If bred long enough and with enough consistency, albinos appear in nearly any species of fish. It is almost always a simple recessive trait, so it is mere child's play to breed

*True albino oscars are actually quite rare in the hobby.*

and perpetuate such a strain once the "sport" appears. The only problem is that albinos are occasionally infertile. Additionally, there are three recognized sub-strains of the albino oscar: the albino red, albino tiger, and snow oscars. Essentially, the main difference between them is the amount of red that they exhibit.

Albino tiger oscars have a defined reddish tiger-like pattern while the albino red oscars have a bright reddish pink solid coloration. The snow oscar usually has a solid white color with an almost yellow dorsal stripe running from nose to tail.

Recently, a new trend has developed with tropical fishes, including oscars—dying them pretty colors. Essentially, dying fishes is done to provide hobbyists with new and exciting colors, like purple, of their favorite species. There are two main problems with this, however. First, the fish must be exposed to what's generally referred to as "acid wash," which melts the protective slime coating off of them so the dye can take hold. Second, the dye wears off after time so you're left with a drab-colored fish with almost no color at all in the end. So, if you ever wondered what a "blueberry" or "raspberry" oscar was, now you know. You will notice that black and orange oscars show up close to Halloween, and red and green oscars show up around Christmas time.

## Sunshine Oscars

These are basically gold oscars that have a high amount of yellow pigmentation, which is usually restricted to the lower half of the body. Sometimes, this yellow pigmentation is very intense and fish exhibiting such intensely colored bellies are referred to as "yellow bellied oscars."

## Zebra Oscars

These are oscars that have noticeable stripes that run from top to bottom.

SMALL FRY

### Colors Change

Baby oscars are patterned very differently from juveniles and adults. Depending on which strain you are keeping, the babies may be drastically different. For example, juvenile wild-type oscars are a deep brown, almost black, in color with an irregular network of creamy streaks all over the body. As the babies grow, the streaks gradually disappear and are replaced by the basic brownish-red adult coloration. While juveniles may be less colorful compared to adults, there's no mistaking them for being oscars!

*This little beauty is a veiltailed albino tiger oscar.*

Often, *A. crassipinnis* is called the zebra oscar but so are specimens of *A.* sp. "Sao Paolo" that originate from Brazil. Common names can be very confusing and rather unclear at times.

## Veiltails Unveiled

In addition to the copious numbers of oscar strains, many of them come in a long-finned form referred to as veiltails. These oscars have fins that vary in length. There are medium veiltails and long veiltails, which many people simply find too much to handle.

While they have never really found a regular following, their popularity spiked after their introduction many years ago and occasionally they will be offered in larger pet shops. Adults in good condition are rare. This is mostly due to the fact that they need to be raised alone in order to develop the elaborate finnage that gives them their description. The fins never really seem to flow however, and more or less just trail along behind them in an odd, rigid fashion.

Veiltailed oscars are more prone to fin damage, and consequently fin diseases such as fin and tail rot. Such issues mainly arise from damage to the fins from fighting or scraping on the tank's decorations. Either way, fin diseases are usually secondary and rarely fatal. Of course, in serious infections the fins can be badly scared and may not fully heal, thus leaving the fins looking ragged and worn.

## A Species Question

As you know from reading chapter one, there are two valid species of oscars: *Astronotus ocellatus* and *A. crassipinnis*. However, over the years a number of other "nominal" species have been suggested. Of these, only one has any merit—*A. orbiculatus*. Described by Haseman in 1911, the type locality is listed as Santerem, Brazil. Two specimens were collected, each at about 5.5 inches (14 cm), which would make them about half grown. Several supporters have offered their reasons for why this fish should be the next valid *Astronotus*. These include: a shallower, more torpedo-like body compared to *A. ocellatus* and *A. crassipinnis*, an absence of dorsal ocelli, a presence of four irregular black bands along the flanks, and having less orange in the fish overall. It should be reinforced that all of this was based on one description of two specimens—either way not nearly enough is known

## Mix & Match

Oscars are oscars and they all basically need the same care. In very large aquariums, hobbyists have successfully kept several oscars of varying color strains together. Ironically, some of these hobbyists report that when multiple specimens of the same strain are kept together with multiple specimens of a different strain, they will stay more closely associated with members of their own strain. Regardless, they can all be kept together with little difficulties other than those imposed by space and food restraints.

to be considered for an argument for, or against, this "new" species.

### How Many?

Today, *Astronotus* is generally referred to as a complex of species. Some ichthyologists have suggested that there are about four species present within it, while others speculate that there may be as many as ten throughout South America. It is now considered common knowledge that there are at least two more species, or possible subspecies, so the number four may be a good start.

Who Am I?

# Chapter 7

# Breeding & Beyond

Hopefully, your love and fascination of oscars will not end with just a simple setup and a lone oscar, as there is so much more to the hobby than what's actually kept in just one aquarium. This chapter is meant to provide a brief introduction to other areas of interest that you can become exposed to (i.e., breeding your oscars, various clubs, and fish shows).

## Breeding Your Oscars!

Given a mature male and female and a big enough aquarium, it is not too difficult to get oscars to spawn. Many hobbyists have done it simply by providing the room and letting nature take its course. The hardest part about breeding oscars, however, is making sure that you actually have a compatible pair and that they have enough room to carry out the spawning process.

## Obtaining a Pair

As far as making sure that you have a pair is concerned, the standard practice followed with many other aquarium fishes—obtaining about a dozen or so young fish and let them grow up together, hoping that the mathematical probability of there being at least one pair of the fish chosen will be high—is tough to follow with fish as big as mature Oscars. You will have to devote too much space to their keeping and wait too long. Oscars won't spawn much before they're about 6 in. (15 cm), which should be when they are about a year to a year-and-a-half old, but many are that size at six months of age because they are fed too much!

Tying up all that tank space for that long can be trying for the prospective oscar breeder and most hobbyists simply don't want to wait that long, so they have to cast about for alternative methods of obtaining breeding-size oscars. If money is no problem, it's easy: all you have to do is buy two obviously fully mature oscars and hope that they're a pair and that if they are a pair, that they're a compatible pair. This latter point is important, because oscars can be

*Juvenile oscars will be sexually mature at the end of their first year.*

*Sexing oscars is difficult at best. Buy a few and let them pair off on their own.*

choosy about their mates. Although they are polygamous and willing to switch mates on the basis of mate availability, not every male is going to be compatible with every female and vice versa, regardless of how good the conditions you provide are. Or at least, not every male and female will be compatible when you want them to be compatible!

A prospective spawning partner might be ignored or fought with four times in a row and then on the fifth they'll successfully spawn, but those first attempts may be very frustrating—enough to even make you want to give up, but never give up! There would be far fewer problems if oscars were able to be sexed reliably, because then all you would have to do is raise up one good fish to maturity, determine its sex, and then scout up a partner of the opposite sex for it.

## Sexing Mature Oscars

You might have read, or been told, that an adult male oscar has a number of spots at the base of his dorsal fin and that a mature female oscar does not, and you might proceed to obtain mature fish that exhibit these differences between one another, figuring to set them up and wait for them to breed after you've provided the best of conditions for them. And you might be very sadly disappointed when nothing at all happens, because the presence or lack of markings on the dorsal fin is simply not a reliable method of determining the sex of any oscar. Some males have them and some males don't, and the same applies to

*Once a pair has formed, they should be given their own tank.*

females. Mature males are sometimes said to be more colorful and more belligerent than mature females; some are and some aren't. In fact, sometimes mature females are downright nasty, as sometimes mature males are, too. Even if size were a completely reliable barometer of sex between fish of the same age, you could only use it with fishes whose age you knew for sure. Size can be as much a product of good feeding regimens and tank accommodations as it is of sex, and so can color—distinctions like these should not be followed blindly as you'll end up wasting a lot of time and money. Additionally, it can be dangerous to count on a difference in size as a guide to the sex of an oscar,

because oscars have a tendency to bully one another, and a much smaller oscar cooped up with a larger one in a tank intended for breeding can get badly mauled or even killed.

## A Few Breeding Situations

Let's cover three specific situations and develop what is considered to be sensible recommendations about how to obtain a male and female oscar for breeding purposes.

### Situation #1

In the first situation, you have only one fish and, judging by the size of the fish, you are pretty sure— or think you know— what its age is and that it is breedable, but you don't know its sex.

Since you don't know the sex of the other oscars you might see, either, you have to cast around a little bit and trust to luck. Breedable oscars are generally expensive, and you don't want to keep trying without success, so it will pay for you to keep the number of introduced prospective mates as small as possible.

## The Hard Part

The first thing you should do is try to find someone in your area who maintains that he has a good record of success in sexing oscars. This person, who may be either an experienced local aquarist or a dealer, may be dead wrong about his ability to differentiate the sexes in oscars, but you still have nothing to lose in letting him pick a mate for your fish…and if he's right you can be saving yourself a lot of trouble and expense. Let him see your fish, and then let him sell you one of his own or pick one out from someone else's stock. Take the hoped-for mate home and, after observing all commonsense aquarium practice precautions such as avoiding temperature differentials, etc., put it into the tank with your oscar.

## Provide a Partition!

Make sure that the tank is partitioned before placing the new oscar in the tank. You will want them to be able to see each other but not get at each other, not yet anyway. If the two oscars indeed constitute a pair, this enforced separation will make them more compatible when they finally do get together. Feed them well while they're separated (a week's separation is about right), and gradually raise the

*Breeder oscars can be very expensive, and you don't want to keep trying without success, so keep the number of prospective mates to a minimum.*

water temperature to 83°F (27°C), keeping it at that point after you have removed the partition.

## Observation

Observe the pair and wait to see what happens. If nothing interesting takes place and the pair just basically ignores each other, then it could be that they're not a pair at all, or that they are a pair but just not ready for spawning, in which case you may want to try partitioning them again for another week or even two. If nothing happens after the second partitioning treatment, or even a third, you may want to start looking for a new potential mate for your fish. You always run the risk of acting too quickly, which is why a third or even a fourth partitioning treatment may be needed, but you don't want to spend too much time in trying to coax a reluctant pair-that-might-not-be-a-pair, either.

If nothing as satisfying as egg-laying happens, but the fish engage in a lot of jaw locking and head-to-tail quivering and tail-slapping, coupled with some very exciting gravel moving

(if there's gravel in the tank) or rock cleaning, then your fish are probably on the right track. Give fish that act this way a day to consummate their pre-spawning roughhouse and housekeeping activities, but if they haven't spawned within a day or so after introducing them, partition them once more. They are close to getting down to business but if failure to spawn persists, then unfortunately you should think about trying yet another fish in replacement of this one. This type of back and forth is fun and exciting for some hobbyists but down-right frustrating for many others; it's all a part of breeding oscars, and you'll have to just be patient while it all works out.

*A female tiger oscar watches over her eggs closely.*

*Oscars will invert themselves and clean the area where spawning will commence.*

If the oscars are openly antagonistic to one another, with one obviously trying to punish the other by biting and butting in the mid-section and around the head, and one fish succeeds in more or less cornering its tankmate, returning every once in a while to deliver a bite or butt, split them up and partition them again. They might be a pair, but most likely they're not; and even if they are, they're not yet ready to spawn. Spawning play among oscars is usually accompanied by a good deal of piscine agonistic behavior, but it's not usually vicious, and the struggle doesn't become lopsided, with one fish doing all of the punishing and the other continuously on the receiving end. If after they've been partitioned and put together again, no improvement is seen in their behavior, keep your fish and return the other one. They are not going to spawn.

### Get Ready!

A telltale sign that a given oscar is ready to spawn is the emergence of its spawning tube, or genital papillae, which consists of an ovipositor in females and sperm chute (or duct) in males. The female's spawning tube is broader and blunter compared to that of the male's because comparatively large eggs must be able to pass through it. If you observe the protrusion of the spawning tube on any of the fish in any of the situations described above, don't be too quick to give up on your chances of eventually being able to obtain a spawn, regardless of how the fish behave when first introduced.

## Situation #2

In the second situation, you have at least two fish of your own that you consider to be a breedable size. You can then just follow the procedure outlined previously, but you can take more time, because you don't have to return any fish to someone else. If you have more than two fish, you can just keep trying various combinations in succession until you find one that works. If you have three oscars, then the odds are pretty good that you'll have a pair. The larger the number of fish you have, the greater the chances necessarily are of obtaining at least one pair; with nine fish, for example, you have almost mathematical certainty that you will have at least one pair. This fact is the single greatest advantage, as far as success in breeding oscars is concerned, in raising your own breeding stock from young fish you acquire. Not many hobbyists,

though, are able to use this system, because of the demands in tank space that such a group of spawning candidates would make.

## Situation #3

The third situation would be one under which you have no oscars at all and must start from scratch to obtain a pair. You can either buy a group of mature oscars at random or buy (or borrow) what someone may claim to be a guaranteed mated pair. Now a guaranteed mated pair is a pair that has proven that they're a pair by spawning and producing viable fry; it is not, however, a pair that is guaranteed to spawn for you when they're in your care. Often, simply moving a

*Once the eggs are laid, you're better off not placing your hands into the aquarium unless there is an emergency.*

*Oscars will most often lay their eggs on flat surfaces. In this case, a piece of slate was used.*

pair will throw their spawning cycle off for several months, so even if you are fortunate enough to get something of the sort, be aware that it may not happen instantaneously. After all, the provider of such a pair is guaranteeing that they are a pair, not that they will actually spawn!

## The Spawning Process

Thus far we haven't covered the actual mechanics of oscar reproduction, so let's do it now. Oscars reproduce in this way: the female lays eggs and the male fertilizes them. Given the proper conditions, tiny fry will emerge from a good number of the fertilized eggs. Some of these fry will die almost immediately; some will linger a few days and then die; some will stay alive for a few weeks or months and then die; and some will survive to maturity. In nature, probably upwards of 90 percent of the fry will die before they reach an inch (2.5 cm) in length; a good number of the remaining ones will die before they ever reach maturity. Basically, you're going to lose a lot of young fish from any spawning, but you should be able to do much better by your oscars compared to nature

## *The Pre-spawning Ritual*

Before the eggs are laid, male and female oscars go through a more or less ritualized series of prespawning motions that may consist of jaw-locking, tail-slapping, chasing and retreating, nipping, threatening,

## The Allure of Spawning Oscars

Part of the aquarists' fascination in breeding oscars is the overwhelming sense of accomplishment that comes along with it, especially if the oscars were raised from babies themselves and spawned by the same hobbyist.

nudging, rolling over....you name it. It may consist of all these things, a few of them, or (very rarely) none of them. Interspersed with the prespawning ritual, which may last from just a few minutes to over a day, will be periods during which either one or both fish settle down to some cleaning of the area which will be the eventual site for depositing the eggs. The area will get a good scrubbing by the fish's mouth. The site for the eggs may be either the bottom of the tank itself or a piece of rockwork in the tank. The rockwork may be either natural, such as a fairly flat piece of shale, or manufactured, such as a slab of slate. If the bottom of the tank is covered with gravel, the fish will clear the gravel away and create a bare spot; they never lay their eggs directly on the gravel. After the egg site has been cleaned to their satisfaction, the female will then deposit her eggs. The eggs will be laid in strings or rows that generally follow a round pattern; that is, the pattern of the egg mass when finally laid will be roughly circular. There is no completely orderly arrangement of the eggs, and about the only thing you can count on is that no egg will be laid on top of a previously laid egg. The eggs will not be laid all at once. Instead, the female will take periodic breathers from her task, and each time she moves away from the egg site the male will come to it and fertilize the eggs.

## Caring for the Eggs

After all of the eggs have been laid and fertilized, the parents normally will settle down to the job of tending them. This job consists primarily of hovering over the eggs, fanning them with their fins and occasionally mouthing them. The fanning keeps water moving over the eggs, thereby keeping them oxygenated and preventing sediment from settling on them; the mouthing also helps keep them clean but also turns up bad eggs and removes them so they don't contaminate the good ones.

Maintained at the same temperature at which the spawning took place, the eggs should hatch within a day and a half or two days. Oscar fry are comparatively large by aquarium fish

*Young oscars will grow very quickly if cared for properly.*

standards but are nonetheless helpless, since they are still not able to swim; they adhere to the spot at which the eggs were hatched, wriggling away in a quivering clump. The parents attend to them continuously.

The fry at this stage require no food, as they still have attached to them the yolk sac, which nourishes them through their first few days of life. The yolk sac usually has been used up within four days of the time the fry have hatched, and at this point the fry become free swimming. They are not good swimmers at first, making feeble darting motions rather than actually swimming, but they are at least no longer confined to one well-defined spot in the tank and completely

SMALL FRY

### A Lifetime Hobby

When children get involved with any type of tropical fish, they often become lifetime aquarists. They may take time off for schooling in their teens and young adult years, but the usually return once they start a family, where they can share the passion with their kids—thus the hobby continues!

dependent on the parent fish for any movement they require. They now need lots of food, and it has to be the right type of food. If given a good diet and frequent feeding, combined with regular large-scale water changes of course, the fry will grow very rapidly. Also, they will be able to take better care of themselves as they get older.

## Another Option

The previous rough chronology of events in the spawning tank assumes that the parents have been left with the eggs. However, it is not necessary to leave the parents with the eggs, because aeration can take the place of the parents fanning the eggs with their fins, and a good fungicide—like methylene blue—can take the place of the parents mouthing efforts. The decision to leave the parents with the eggs or remove the parents depends on

### Sharing the Passion

Conventions of national fish clubs are a way for large numbers of aquarists to have fun, learn, and share their passion for their fish.

what you value more, the spectacle of watching the parents care for their young, or a guarantee that the eggs will not be actually eaten by the parents, which happens especially frequently with new oscar parents. For even though oscars are generally good parents, one or both of them might somewhere along the lines eat the eggs…or the fry.

If you're determined to get baby oscars do it this way: if the eggs have been laid on a rock or piece of slate, remove the egg-bearing object and place it into a non-toxic receptacle big enough to cover the eggs to a depth of 6 in. (15 cm) or so and leave a good 4 to 5 in. (10 to 12.5 cm) all around the object. If the eggs are on a thin slab, prop something under one side so that the slab will be angled, with the higher end about 2 in. (5 cm) from the bottom. Place an airstone under the high end of the slab and set the aeration release rate so that a steady but not violent stream of air bubbles will rise upward around the eggs. The bubbles should go around, not actually onto the eggs. The water in the hatching receptacle should be taken from the tank in which the parents spawned, and the water should have a good strong solution of methylene blue added to it, enough to turn the water dark blue. Acriflavine also can be used. Keep the temperature steady, and wait for the eggs to hatch. After they hatch, the fry will slowly tumble

*This baby oscar is showing the normal pattern for its size.*

off the slate or whatever they hatched on and fall to the bottom, where they'll wriggle around. Remove the slate when all of the fry have left it. When the fry have lost the yolk sac and actively seek food, feed them.

## Feeding the Fry

Feeding the newly hatched oscar fry is the crucial point in the successful spawning and raising of aquarium fishes. In the raising of most species, the ability, or lack of ability, of the breeder to provide the proper nutrition in a small enough package is directly related to success or failure. If he can provide the oscar fry with good-quality food, he's home free; if he can't, it's all over. Oscar breeders are fortunate however, as baby oscars are easy to feed. They are large enough at the time they need food most to be able to eat newly hatched brine shrimp. They don't need the rotifers and protozoans

that many other tropical fish fry require, and the job of the oscar breeder is thus made easier.

### Baby Brine Shrimp

You can set up as many brine shrimp hatching containers as you need, and you can hatch as many brine shrimp as you need; the only thing it will cost you is money. When you consider the job they do for you, brine shrimp eggs are not expensive at all, really, and the little pink crustaceans that hatch from them will prove themselves invaluable to you in your task of getting oscar babies past their first few crucial weeks. You're going to lose some of the fry regardless of how well you feed them. Brine shrimp eggs vary in quality as to both percentage of hatch and the size of the nauplii; try different brands of eggs from different areas to see which work best for you.

### The Brine Shrimp Hatchery

Brine shrimp hatchery units are available commercially, but most hobbyists usually use wide-mouth glass jars instead. The jars, filled half-way to two-thirds their capacity with brine shrimp hatching solution, are tilted on their sides to provide maximum surface area. An airstone put into the jar will provide aeration and brisk agitation, which the brine shrimp need in order to hatch correctly. The eggs will hatch fairly quickly, according to the temperature and salinity of the solution. Follow the directions on the container of the eggs closely for best results.

## Powder, Liquid & Paste Foods

Several types of prepared foods are available for using as a first-food for baby oscars. Of these, the most commonly used is a powder, which is basically a pulverized growth enhancing flake food. Next in popularity is a liquid diet, which is actually more like gel. It falls apart rather quickly so if the oscars don't come right up to it then this food will often cause more major water fouling problems. Lastly there is paste, which

## The Expert Knows

### Shows & Conventions

Club membership often leads aquarists to national and international shows and conventions, though many of the attendees at these events are not members of a local aquarium club. Typically, activities at the conventions feature three or more days of presentations, workshops, and panel discussions, punctuated with plenty of fun activities, socializing, and fish sales. In effect, conventions are mega-scale club meetings. The same benefits accrue, only expanded to national and international levels.

is quite popular but a bit messy. Discus breeders use pastes very often and there are many types. Also, quite a few dedicated hobbyists actually make their own pastes. This way, the ingredients can be varied to suit the needs of the particular species you're raising on them.

## Clubs

One of the best ways to network with other hobbyists, who may or may not share your enthusiasm for oscars, is to join a fish club or society. Often, there are clubs that are closer than you may think, and best of all, there are more people that attend them than you probably think.

## Fish & Supplies

The big clubs have big auctions, and you can often find oscars at these events. Additionally, some of the rarest fish in the world can be found only at these big national sales.

*An adult tiger oscar is always a pleasure to observe.*

The best way to grow in the aquarium hobby is to join an aquarium society. There is sure to be one closer than you think.

Additionally, there are specialized clubs: there are livebearer clubs, cichlid clubs, killifish clubs, koi clubs, and many others. You don't just have to belong to one club; you can belong to many clubs.

## Speakers

Speakers from around the world come together to give the latest news, updates on scientific matters, and reports of collecting expeditions. Often there are so many speakers that two or three sessions run simultaneously. In addition, many national clubs are actively involved in conservation, and they often have fundraising events that finance both conservation and scientific research. These feed back into the organization, and, in turn, educate the members.

There are many opportunities at these conventions to speak one-on-one with some of the most prominent experts in the field and to get answers to your questions and suggestions for your fishroom.

# Resources

## Magazines

**Tropical Fish Hobbyist**
1 T.F.H. Plaza
3rd & Union Avenues
Neptune City, NJ 07753
Phone: (732) 988-8400
E-mail: info@tfh.com
www.tfhmagazine.com

## Internet Resources

**A World of Fish**
www.aworldoffish.com

Oscars

**Aquarium Hobbyist**
www.aquariumhobbyist.com

**Cichlidfish.com**
www.cichlidfish.com

**Cichlid Forum**
www.cichlid-forum.com

**Discus Page Holland**
www.dph.nl

**FINS: The Fish Information Service**
http://fins.actwin.com

**Fish Geeks**
www.fishgeeks.com

**Fish Index**
www.fishindex.com

**MyFishTank.Net**
www.myfishtank.net
Oscarfish.com
www.oscarfish.com

**Planet Catfish**
www.planetcatfish.com

**Tropical Resources**
www.tropicalresources.net

**Water Wolves**
http://forums.waterwolves.com

## Associations & Societies

**American Cichlid Association**
Claudia Dickinson, Membership
Coordinator
P.O. Box 5078
Montauk, NY 11954
Phone: (631) 668-5125
E-mail: IvyRose@optonline.net
www.cichlid.org

**American Killifish Association**
Catherine Carney, Secretary
12723 Airport Road
Mt. Vernon, OH 43050
E-mail: schmidtcarney@ecr.net
www.aka.org

**American Livebearer Association**
Timothy Brady, Membership Chairman
5 Zerbe Street
Cressona, PA 17929-1513
Phone: (570) 385-0573
http://livebearers.org

**Association of Aquarists**
David Davis, Membership Secretary
2 Telephone Road
Portsmouth, Hants, England
PO4 0AY
Phone: 01705 798686

**British Killifish Association**
Adrian Burge, Publicity Officer
E-mail: adjan@wym.u-net.com
www.bka.org.uk

**Canadian Association of Aquarium Clubs**
Miecia Burden, Membership
Coordinator
142 Stonehenge Pl.
Kitchener, Ontario, Canada
N2N 2M7
Phone: (517) 745-1452
E-mail: mbburden@look.ca
www.caoac.on.ca

**Canadian Killifish Association**
Chris Sinclair, Membership
1251 Bray Court
Mississauga, Ontario, Canada L5J 354
Phone: (905) 471-8681
E-mail: cka@rogers.com
www.cka.org

**Federation of American Aquarium Societies**
Jane Benes, Secretary
923 Wadsworth Street
Syracuse, NY 13208-2419
Phone: (513) 894-7289
E-mail: jbenes01@yahoo.com
www.gcca.net/faas

**Goldfish Society of America**
P.O. Box 551373
Fort Lauderdale, FL 33355
E-mail: info@goldfishsociety.org
www.goldfishsociety.org

**International Fancy Guppy Association**
Rick Grigsby, Secretary
3552 West Lily Garden Lane
South Jordan, Utah 84095
Phone: (801) 694-7425
E-mail: genx632@yahoo.com
www.ifga.org

**National Aquarium in Baltimore**
501 E. Pratt Street
Baltimore, Maryland 21202.
Phone: (410) 576-3800
www.aqua.org

# Index

Index

# About the Authors

**Neal Pronek** is a pet care expert. He has served as an Assistant Editor, Editor, Managing Editor, and Editor-in-Chief throughout his 40-year career with T.F.H. Publications. Today, Neal is retired and spends his days watching fishes in his home in Farmingdale, New Jersey.

**Brian M. Scott** received his Bachelor of Science degree in biology from the Richard Stockton College of New Jersey in 2001. An avid fishkeeper since childhood, Brian writes a monthly column, "Top of The Food Chain" in *Tropical Fish Hobbyist* Magazine. He maintains several large aquariums in his home in Barnegat, New Jersey—some of which contain oscars.

# Photo Credits
Photos courtesy of TFH Archives

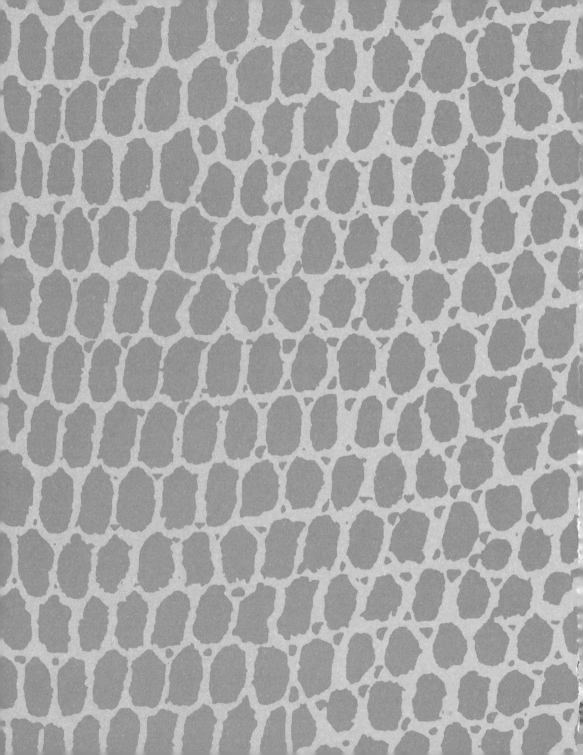